Weight Wisdom

Weight Wisdom

*Affirmations to Free You
from Food and Body Concerns*

Written by
Kathleen Burns Kingsbury, LMHC
&
Mary Ellen Williams, LICSW

Brunner-Routledge
New York and Hove

Published in 2003 by
Brunner-Routledge
29 West 35th Street
New York, NY 10001
www.brunner-routledge.com

Published in Great Britain by
Brunner-Routledge
27 Church Road
Hove, East Sussex
BN3 2FA
www.brunner-routledge.co.uk

Brunner-Routledge is an imprint of the Taylor & Francis Group.
Printed in the United States of America on acid-free paper.

10 9 8 7 6 5 4 3 2 1

Library of Congress Cataloging-in-Publication Data

Kingsbury, Kathleen Burns, 1966–
   Weight wisdom : affirmations to free you from food and body concerns / written
by Kathleen Burns Kingsbury & Mary Ellen Williams.
      p. cm.
Includes bibliographical references.
   ISBN 0-415-94434-1
   1. Eating disorders—Psychological aspects. 2. Body image. 2. Affirmations.
I. Williams, Mary Ellen, 1961–   II. Title.

RC552 . E18K54 2003
616 . 85′ 26—dc21
                                                                    2003002649

Dedication

We dedicate this book to the countless individuals who have shared their recovery stories with us. It is through your willingness to give of yourself and to walk with another on your life's journey that we have prospered. We have been touched by your openness and honored to connect, learn, and grow with you.

Contents

Acknowledgments

Two may have written this book, but it took many to complete. We want to acknowledge all who were involved in the process. We especially wish to thank the following people who supported us and made our dream of a book a reality.

Kathleen wishes to acknowledge:

Brian, my husband, who has allowed me to follow my dream. Your never-ending support, love, and laughter makes every day truly a gift.

My parents who were feminists before their time. Thanks for teaching me that I can be and do anything.

My sister, Laurie, who taught me that life is not a dress rehearsal.

Beth Mayer and Christine Shruhan for modeling what it is to be true to oneself and to one's clients. Your collegial support, mentoring, and friendship are and continue to be invaluable.

Jennifer Campbell, my office assistant, who tirelessly typed and retyped the manuscript. Your enthusiasm and support made the more technical parts of the process fun.

The National Eating Disorders Association, for your enthusiasm, support and contribution to this book.

And most of all, Mary Ellen Williams, who invited me on this journey many years ago. You truly do notice the moon and have taught me to celebrate each victory along the way.

Mary Ellen wishes to acknowledge:

My husband, Tom, for your fervent support which allows me to explore my life's path. Your daily love and acceptance provides the foundation onto which I can grow.

My daughters, Emily and Hannah, thanks for bringing joy and love into my life and for constantly reminding me of the importance of play.

My mother, Mary, siblings, Diane, Patty, and Jim, and especially my deceased father, Jim, for your sense of humor, generosity, and appreciation of life's simple pleasures for which this book beholds so much of your spirit.

To my friend and mentor, Deborah Bluestone, for your steadfast friendship, editorial and technical feedback, and encouragement.

To my co-author, Kathleen, for always being the other half on this project. Your ability and willingness to do so was the wind that made this project sail.

To my child-care providers, Michelle, Jessie, and Jessica, for your loving care of my children, as we wrote this book.

To my colleagues associated with the Massachusetts Eating Disorders Association and the South Shore Eating Disorders Collaborative, many of whom taught me by their experience and supported us during various phases of this book.

Finally, to the many other colleagues, supervisors, lecturers, and individuals that have shared so much of their work, knowledge, and life struggles with me. Your willingness to share yourself has been significant, touching, and inspirational.

Introduction

When we started to write *Weight Wisdom,* we wanted to reach out to the many women* who are unhappy with their relationship with food. Women who are tired of dieting, tired of obsessing about calories and fat grams, and sick of working out when their bodies tell them to rest. Women who are abusing their bodies by bingeing and purging, restricting, using laxatives, diet pills, and diet supplements. Women who believe life would be so much easier if they could only achieve their "ideal weight." If this is you, someone you love, or someone you are treating in your psychotherapy practice, we are glad you have found this book!

Through our training and countless journeys with those who suffer from eating disorders, we have found people who often have similar thoughts and beliefs about food, weight, diet, and exercise. These thoughts and beliefs are called cognitive distortions or irrational beliefs. They are learned from families, peers, and society, and are reinforced by experiences in the world. Cognitive distortions perpetuate food and weight concerns. *Weight Wisdom* is written to help you identify and change the belief system that supports your unhealthy eating behaviors. For this is the key to ending your battle with food.

Our first lessons about food, weight, and body acceptance come from our families. From the time we are infants, our caregivers teach us how to eat, how to respond to (or ignore) our hunger, and how to love and appreciate our body. These lessons are integrated into our thought process and stay with us into adulthood. Some families have taught healthy messages, such as that food is fuel. Other families, have

---

*While we use "woman" throughout the book, we realize many men struggle with food issues and eating disorders as well. This book is not meant to be exclusive. Ninety percent of individuals in treatment for eating disorders are female and therefore, we chose to use the female pronoun throughout the book. Our hope is that men who are also affected by this problem, will also read the book and find it useful.

taught inaccurate information about food, weight, and exercise, such as the belief that eating less food makes you a better person.

Our diet-crazed society reinforces many of the unhealthy messages we have received as children. How many diet ads have you seen that tell you that if you lost weight you would be a better, happier person? Daily, we are bombarded with thousands of media messages—television and print advertisements, magazine articles, and beauty industry billboards. These media outlets tell us what to think, feel, and believe about thinness, attractiveness, and success. If we eat fat-free food, we are "good"; if we give in to a chocolate craving, we are "bad."

Last and most important, our experiences in the world either reinforce or question the paradigms we learn from our family and our culture. When we experience an event as affirming what we were taught to be true, we then internalize it, and the thought becomes a part of our personal belief system. For most individuals who struggle with eating concerns, these thoughts and beliefs are inaccurate and distorted. They fuel the disordered eating behaviors and block full recovery. If we believe that our self-worth is determined by our dress size, then our dress size will determine our self-worth.

The good news is that these distorted beliefs can be unlearned and replaced with healthier, more accurate thoughts. First we must identify the distorted thinking that fosters starvation dieting, binge eating, purging, and excessive exercising. Second we need to replace this "stinking thinking" with rational reasoning. *Weight Wisdom* is designed to help you do just that.

Recovery is not a destination. It is a personal journey on a long and winding road with many twists and turns along the way. While many search for books, therapists, and other sources for the magic answer or a quick fix to their eating issues, those who have recovered fully will tell you that recovery is a process. As clinicians trained to help you navigate this road, we are providing you with guidelines and tips based on our experience in the eating disorders field. This book is your road map with points of special interest and traveling tips. Three of the book's sections represent the typical challenges at the beginning, middle, and end stages of recovery. Each section contains reflections applicable to a particular leg of the journey. Section One, *The Journey Begins . . .* is dedicated to basic tenets of recovery. Section Two, *Conquering the Hills and Valleys* discusses how to work on the issues that are underlying your food and weight obsession while coping with the inevitable frustrations of the process. Section Three, *Continuing the Journey . . .* addresses how to continue this personal growth and practice these techniques for a lifetime of recovery. As this expedition is uniquely yours, we encourage you to be an active participant in the process. At the end of each entry, we have provided a helpful hint. You can use these hints to further explore the book's concepts and to make them your own.

We have included Section Four, *The Loved One's Journey,* and Section Five, *The Professional's Journey,* to coach the support people you choose to be helpful and effective. As with any trip, traveling with someone can be useful. If you do not already have a therapist, you may want to consider finding one. Another excellent travel companion is a support group. Not unlike a guided tour, the group and its leader will accompany you to unexplored places. The leader provides guidance and education, while the group members, like fellow tourists, discover the sights along with you and marvel at what is learned. If you need help locating a therapist and/or a support group in your area, we have included guidelines for finding a qualified counselor and a list of treatment resources section.

As you travel on your journey, we wish you the best. Be aware that the many tips contained in the book are intended to be tools. As with any project, you determine which tools to use, when to use them, and when to store them in your toolbox. Some you will keep for life, and some you will leave along the road. This is okay as you alone are the creator of your road map to recovery.

The Journey Begins . . .

You're Not Crazy, You're Coping.

"I must be nuts," Claire said as she sat on the couch in my office. "I can't handle stress without bingeing. I can't tell you what I am feeling and most of the time I feel numb." It was our first meeting, and Claire had described a childhood of physical and verbal abuse, dieting, and overeating. Food was her constant companion. It was her friend. She could count on it when she could not rely on her alcoholic father or her distant mother to comfort her. I looked at Claire and smiled. I said gently, "You're not crazy, you're coping." Food was stable, safe, and reliable when her parents were not. When she was scared of her father as a kid, she would eat. As an adult, when she was scared, she would binge. It made sense to her. "Yeah, I guess you are right. I am not crazy, I am coping!"

Like many women with food issues, Claire blamed herself for using food to get her through difficult times. She called herself names, put herself down, and repeated in her head what she so often heard as a child—that she was worthless. With support and guidance, Claire was able to see her symptoms as coping strategies. "Boy, I must have been pretty smart to use food this way. My sister turned to drugs, and my brother used violence."

Yes, Claire, like many women, was brilliant in her way of dealing with an abusive childhood. Discovering how your symptoms helped you grow up in a dysfunctional family or handle day-to-day life problems, is vital in recovery. Symptoms need to be respected and appreciated as ingenious ways of getting through tough times. If you are reading this book, you are probably ready to develop healthier ways of coping with stress, anger, fear, sadness, and other difficult feelings.

Healthier techniques such as assertiveness skills, affect management, conflict negotiation, and self-love can be learned. The first step in that learning process is to stop calling your self "crazy." Instead of name-calling, pat yourself on the back. Give yourself credit for taking the first and often most challenging step of admitting you have a problem with food. Instead of calling yourself "crazy" yell out, *"I am not crazy, I am coping!"*

Food Log:

Date	Food/Drink	Binge?/Purge?	Thoughts/Feelings
4/22	cookies	yes/yes	I blew my diet. Shame

There Is No Magic Wand.

How many times have we heard the same question: "Do you have the magic wand?" A person sits and asks us during our first meeting with her eyes wide with anticipation, hopeful we will be the one with the answer to her eating concern. Each time we tell the individual that there is no magic wand for recovery, we watch the hope vanish from her face as her body sinks in the chair.

In a society of fast food, quick weight loss schemes, and instant gratification, it is difficult to learn that there is no quick fix for eating disorders. In fact, the recovery process is slow, long, and often painful. But it can also bring joy, delight, and a sense of self-confidence never felt before. We do not have the magic wand, you do. The magic wand is within you. You just need to find it and learn to use it.

That is what this book is about. It is about finding out what works for you and what doesn't. It is discovering the color, shape, size, and texture of your own personal wand of recovery. For you do have the power to get well. But only you, often with the help of a good therapist, physician, support group, and/or friend, can discover your true authentic self. While the process of finding, building, and using the magic wand (recovery) is long, it is a lot more rewarding than a quick fix. It will survive the test of time, and is far more fulfilling than the empty promise you will get from your local diet center or nutrition store.

Helpful Hint:

> Make your own magic wand. Use clay, crayons, paper,
> material, or any art supplies to make a magic wand of your
> very own. What color, texture, shape, and size would it be?
> What qualities do you have inside you that will make your
> magic wand work? What are your strengths? How can you
> incorporate these strengths into your artistic representation
> of your magic wand? Be creative!

Find a Safe Place to Heal.

Weight Wisdom was written to provide inspiration to our readers. If reading this book is your first step in recovery, we are thrilled that you found it. If you have been working toward recovery for a while, we hope this book provides reflections, which will be useful in your work. It was not our intent for *Weight Wisdom* to be your only source of treatment. Full recovery from most food and weight concerns requires professional help. Therefore, we strongly recommend that, if you have not done so already, you enlist an eating disorders professional to conduct a thorough psychological and medical assessment.

An assessment may include a physician, a psychiatrist, a psychologist, a licensed counselor or social worker, and a nutritionist. Due to the fact that an eating disorder is a multifaceted problem, all of these aspects of your health need to be evaluated. Once this assessment is complete, a professional will help you identify the underlying issues that led you to disordered eating. The clinician will collaborate with you in developing a treatment plan and treatment team that will best meet your needs. It is vital that you feel comfortable with your treatment providers, especially your individual therapist. While the therapeutic work will at times cause discomfort, the personal match with your therapist should not. As with anything new, give it some time. But if you go for a few sessions and do not feel like it is a good match, talk to the therapist and/or other treatment team members about finding a better fit.

As your treatment progresses, you will discover therapy can be a safe place to heal. The therapist will become a support and provide a place to talk about your relationship with food without judgment or criticism. He or she can offer education to you and to your family, teaching your loved ones how to best support you during this healing process. The clinician will provide important links to resources in your local area. But most of all, a trained therapist will help you develop and practice the skills discussed in this book and incorporate them into your daily life.

While starting therapy can be intimidating in the beginning, it often becomes a safe place for you to share your fears, worries, and victories during your recovery. Due to the denial inherent in the illness, it is best not to be the only judge of the seriousness of your problem. Many people feel weak if they need help to get better. But it shows strength, not weakness, to seek professional care. It takes courage to pick up the telephone, call your doctor or local eating disorders referral agency, and ask for help. It is unrealistic to do it alone. So find a safe place to heal. The road to recovery is best traveled with a companion.

Helpful Hint:

Review the questionnaire entitled "Do I have an eating disorder?" found in the resource section of this book. Based on the results, make an appointment for an assessment with an eating disorders professional in your area. If you do not know where to find help, refer to the resource list.

It Is Not Your Weight,
It Is the Weight of Your Issues.

Why do people develop eating disorders? Simply put, they develop the symptoms in attempting to solve a problem. It may be that they use restriction, dieting, or bingeing to cope with difficult feelings or situations in life. Feelings such as sadness, loneliness, anger, and fear are burdensome, heavy emotions. These feelings can make us believe we weigh a million pounds. We falsely believe that if we focus on reducing our weight or changing our body size and shape, we will feel lighter. However, the burden of our issues remains unchanged.

If you are new to the recovery process, you may still see your weight as the problem. Well-meaning friends and family members may reinforce this idea by commenting and worrying about your weight and your symptoms rather than about the underlying causes of your struggle. You and your support system need to learn that the real road to recovery has much less to do with your physical weight than it does with the emotional weight of the psychological issues you have or are currently facing.

Let's take an example all can relate to. How many people do you know who have gone on a diet after the breakup of a romantic relationship? Losing someone is heavy stuff. The pain of the loss may feel like a big boulder sitting in your stomach. Only time will make the boulder of sadness shrink. In a society of quick fixes, we seldom wait for feelings to pass naturally. We get busy buying the latest diet book, going to the gym, and skipping meals with the hope that by reducing our dress size, our dating quotient will increase and the pain will end. However, the heaviness in our stomach remains until the time necessary to heal has passed.

A diet does not ease emotional pain. Instead, it is a poor temporary distraction. In the short run it may help us forget the pain of our loss, but when the diet is broken or the weight does not come off, we feel worse. The pain of the loss is compounded by the negative feelings associated with falling off the diet wagon. The only way through a feeling is to feel it. Time needs to pass. Emotions need to settle and dissipate. Your heart needs to heal. There is no way to reduce the pain involved in being a human being. The answer lies in recognizing, examining, and coming to peace with the emotionally laden problems of living.

Helpful Hint:

The next time you start worrying about your weight, stop and ask yourself the following question: If I was not worried about my weight, what would I be worried about? Often our discomfort about life gets projected onto to our physical body. Asking this one question is a great technique to help you start identifying the "weighty issues" you may need to address in therapy.

If Thin Is In, I Don't Want to Win.

There is an assumption in our society that thin people are healthier than fat people. The diet industry fuels this belief, while the medical profession often reinforces it. The trouble with this way of thinking is that it does not consider the whole person. Other factors, besides the number on the scale, must be considered in assessing someone's health. These other factors include a person's cardiovascular strength, nutrition, physical fitness, blood pressure, cholesterol level, and emotional well-being. While these items do not show up on the scale each morning, they are a big part of your overall health.

Many people, especially those with food and weight concerns, battle weight concerns with the belief that those who are the thinnest win. The old saying "You can never be too rich or too thin" becomes a personal mantra. But what are the costs of trying to be the thinnest? Whether you struggle with anorexia, bulimia, binge eating, or you find that you are perpetually dieting and worried about your weight, the costs are great. The medical risks associated with anorexia include emaciation, slow heart rate, low blood pressure, gastrointestinal disorders, menstrual irregularities including amenorrhea, loss of muscle tissue, osteoporosis, altered brain function and size, anemia, and impaired renal function. The medical complications from bulimia include fluid and electrolyte imbalances, tooth decay and gum erosion, enlargement of saliva glands, esophagus tears or ruptures, gastrointestinal disorders, muscular weakness (remember your heart is a muscle!), edema, vitamin deficiency, and central nervous system disturbances. With binge eating disorders, some of the risks are the same, but also include diabetes, heart disease, and high blood pressure. The ultimate risk of any eating problem is death. Eating disorders have the highest mortality rate of any psychiatric illness!

Why don't people with eating concerns just stop their behaviors once they realize the medical and emotional tolls they entail? Eating disorders occur on a continuum from chronic dieting to food and weight obsessions to life-threatening anorexia and bulimia. The more severe the eating disorder, the less concerned one is likely to be about her physical health. The illness distorts how one thinks about medical problems. Some people even go so far as to use the medical side effects as a measure of success, believing statements like "If I am not at death's door, than I am not a good anorexic."

Due to the denial factor and the medical risks involved, professionals and support systems need to monitor the unhealthy behaviors you are engaging in, as they can be dangerous. Routine visits to the doctor are important. Eventually, with help, you will realize the risks are too great, and you are worth too much to continue your unhealthy behaviors. Do you really want to play the game of Russian roulette?

Life is better when you learn to accept your natural weight. By no longer engaging in dangerous dieting habits, you avoid all the medical complications and restore your physical and mental health. So next time someone tells you that you can never be too thin, yell back, "If thin is in, I don't want to win!"

Helpful Hint:

Make an appointment with a physician, nurse practitioner, or physician's assistant who is educated about eating disorders. Have a full physical examination. If you are uncomfortable with your current doctor, call one of the national eating disorders organizations in the resource section for referrals in your area.

You Are Not Your Dress Size.

The day Oprah Winfrey, a successful talk show host, wealthy business-woman, and talented actor, pulled a wagon full of fat onto stage and exclaimed, "This is the happiest day of my life," was a sad day for us all. She told the audience she was the proudest of her weight loss than any other accomplishment in her life.

Oprah, like many women struggling with food and weight concerns, missed the point. She had mistaken her physical size as a measure of her success. She had confused her self-worth with her dress size. Since that time, Oprah regained and lost the weight again. Over time, she has discovered dieting is not the answer and has found a better-balanced program of self-care, which includes exercise, healthy eating, and spirituality.

Many women with food and weight concerns confuse personal happiness with fitting into a size 6, 10, or 18 dress. They forget that their physical appearance is only one aspect of who they are as a person. Many forget that regardless of the size on the tag, they are needed as mothers, wives, lovers, and friends. They forget that their contribution to the world has much more to do with who they are as people than it does with what they look like to others.

When was the last time you picked a friend or a business associate based on the size of their clothes? Do you even know the size of your friends' and associates' clothing? In most instances, probably not. It sounds absurd to judge others in this way, but every day millions of women judge themselves by these arbitrary numbers. We often learn to ignore our special internal qualities such as kindness, compassion, intelligence, wit, and perseverance, when evaluating our worth.

So the next time you look in the mirror and say to yourself that you are a bad person for not fitting into your "thin" clothes, remember you are not your dress size. And by the way, throw out the "thin" clothes while you are at it!

Helpful Hint:

Research how designers label clothes and determine dress sizes. You might wonder why you are a designer size 12 and a discount department store size 14. It is not a coincidence. It is marketing!

Think Genetics.

Growing up in what was considered the Snow Belt area of Massachusetts, I lived next to a neighbor who plowed snow for a living. On the baby-blue snowplow of her pickup truck she had painted the words *Think Snow.* It made me giggle as a child to consider the inference in her amusing phrase. Even as a child I knew that forecasting the weather owed more to science than to wishful thinking. After all, in the third grade we learned about the water cycle.

Many men and women, who are pursuing thinness, weight loss, or the perfect body, often rely on unscientific wishful thinking. Many will have images of a beautiful body; with ideal proportions, body parts of a perfect size and shape, or of an all-important number on the scale. They will have hopes, like my childhood neighbor, that their wishful thinking and desire for a particular outcome will magically defy the laws of nature and science. Many will not consider the role of genetics as they pursue their goals. It always amazes us that, although people can generally accept the role of genetics in determining their height, hair color and texture, skin tone, eye color, blood type, intelligence quotient, and various medical conditions, they nonetheless assume genetics has nothing to do with their body weight, shape, or size.

Genetics is a crucial determinate of our body type. We inherit factors which determine our weight range and distribution. These factors are influenced by the size of our bones, the muscle mass needed to move those bones, the number of fat and skin cells needed to protect our skeletal and muscular system, the rate of our metabolism; and by our sex and our age. Genetics, not willpower, wishful thinking, or discipline, controls all these factors. Indeed, we do have some control over the range of our genetically predetermined weight, but it is far more limited than the diet and exercise industry would like us to believe. So as you start your journey, think genetics!

Helpful Hint:

Compose a family tree diagram that is multigenerational. Include parents, siblings, aunts, uncles, grandparents, cousins, and great-grandparents. Track and record a variety of genetic physical traits. Observe similarities that can be attributed to genetics. Notice if you have Uncle Cliff's nose, Grandma Adeline's smile, your mother's shape, or your father's physique.

Recovery Is an Inside Job.

"Lose weight and you will have friends." "Don't wear that, it makes you look fat." "How could you have had that cookie? You blew it again!" The insidious eating disorder voice repeatedly whispers to you that your physical appearance, dress size, weight, or control over your appetite determines your happiness and success in life. This message is mirrored by the thousands of diet advertisements and media images that you see, hear, or read each day. Consequently you may believe that once you reach your ideal weight or achieve the perfect body fat percentage all life has to offer would unfold for your taking. Why not? Isn't that what society promises us?

However, recovery happens on the inside, not the outside. Diets, exercise, and supplements are not going to lead to increased self-worth and a sense of contentment. In fact, this approach often leads to lower self-esteem and self-criticism.

The real work of recovery is not cosmetic. It happens inside where our emotions, family histories, and private thoughts reside. It often involves examining one's lack of self-confidence and where it originated. Do you struggle with depression and anxiety? Have you experienced verbal, physical, or sexual abuse? Did you grow up with an alcoholic, workaholic, or a parent with an eating disorder? All these factors can contribute to the development of disordered eating behaviors. The behavior started as a way to cope with difficulties and ended up a problem in itself.

You may have begun your recovery process hoping that weight loss will result. Do not judge yourself for that wish. It is natural to think this way at the beginning. It is the nature of the problem. As your journey unfolds, you will realize that recovery is really about reaching inside and seeing what emerges. Some of it will be enjoyable. Some of it will be painful and shameful. The key is to have a safe place to tell your story. Whether that is with a trusted friend, with a therapist, or in a support group, it is important that you have a place to share your story and to help you refocus on the internal work when the eating disorder voice longingly calls you back to the superficial.

Helpful Hint:

Create a diet history. On a piece of paper or in a journal,
starting with the first time you worried about your weight,
write down all the times you lost or gained weight, started
or stopped a diet, or became more or less symptomatic. Next
to each mark on your timeline write down what was
happening in your life at the time. This timeline will help
you see how your eating behaviors are tied to what is
happening in your personal and emotional life.

Fat Is Not a Feeling.

"I feel fat," Madeline, a seven-year-old girl, tells her mom as she pulls at her stomach. Her mom had hoped her little girl would not have to deal with food and weight obsession at such a young age. Had she overheard her say similar things about her own body? Madeline had spoken the universal statement of womanhood—"I feel fat!" Unfortunately, it is a national anthem for many women. To be an adult female in our society is often to dislike one's body.

How can we stop this type of body hatred? What can we do to teach our young girls and ourselves to love our bodies? Our physical being is beautiful. It allows us to walk to the store, run on a beach, make love with our partners, and to hold our children. No matter what the size, our bodies help us live. The first step towards ending body shame is to start letting go of the statement "I am fat" and start labeling what is really going on.

"Fat" is not a feeling, but a descriptive term similar to stating that your eyes are blue, you are short, and so on . . . But many women use the "fat word" to describe their sadness, anger, hurt, and exhaustion. Many label themselves "fat" when they are at or below normal weight. They use the word to harshly judge themselves, believing that it will lead to a happier self. Whether you are fat or not, calling yourself names and failing to identify your feelings does not lead to happiness.

By mislabeling feelings as fat, we are negating them, pushing them down. Many starve or stuff these mislabeled feelings with food. The temporary numbness brought on by restricting, bingeing, or purging masks our true emotions. We get distracted and play the game of self-loathing—a game in which we know all the rules. It is a game that feels safe and familiar. The feeling game is more abstract and unpredictable. It may be scary and unfamiliar. So is body hatred or calling yourself fat really a solution to managing problems or just a familiar detour in the road?

Declaring, "I feel fat," is like a war cry against the body. But the body loses the battle. You lose the battle. Learn to tolerate feelings through self-acceptance and self-care. If it is difficult or too scary to do alone, find a good therapist to help you along the way. Whatever the feeling, it will pass, once acknowledged. Stating, "I feel fat," is a cry for help, for validation, or for attention. These are okay things to need and want. So ask for them! Reach out for support next time you feel weighted down by your problems. You may be surprised that accepting the feelings, sitting with them, then letting them pass can make you feel emotionally lighter.

Next time you say, "I am fat," stop and ask yourself what is it that you are really trying to communicate. Do I feel inadequate? Is it fear? Is it anxiety? Am I tired? Maybe it is all these emotions wrapped into one big ball of feeling. This ball you carry makes you feel heavy even though you physically weigh the same as yesterday.

Helpful Hint:

Practice describing your experience without using the word "fat." "I feel fat," may translate into, "I am uncomfortable in my body, and I am tired." Or it may mean, "I feel worthless and unloved." When caught in a cycle of body hatred, ask yourself what do I need today? Is it support, a hug, or a good laugh? Once you discover your needs, find a way to get them met. In the long run, getting your needs met in life goes much further toward happiness than starting a new diet plan today.

The Pyramid Was Not Built in a Day.

"I was so bad yesterday. I ate a pizza and ice cream," Catlin exclaimed as she entered my office for her therapy session. I wondered with her what was so "bad" about pizza and ice cream and how could what she ate make her a bad person. Her eyes got big and she said, "Everyone knows pizza and ice cream are bad foods!"

Do you think like Catlin? Many of us have been brainwashed by diet programs and cultural messages that there are two food groups—good foods and bad foods. Last time I checked there still were six—fruits, vegetables, grains, dairy, fat, and protein. The dreaded food pyramid still lives.

The pyramid was created to teach us some basic tenets of nutrition. These include eating a variety of foods at each meal, eating every three to four hours, and responding to the body's hunger cues. Yes, there is some truth to the food pyramid philosophy! It is important to have mixed meals, including protein, vegetables, grains, fruits, fats, and dairy products. By having a variety of foods, you will satisfy your daily nutritional requirements, as well as feel satisfied. Contrary to the popular diet mentality, a function of eating is to feel satisfied after a meal. Many diet programs lead you to believe that the goal of each meal is to feel good about how little you were able to eat or how few points, calories, or carbohydrates you consumed. Feeling satisfied after meals may take a while if you have been engaging in disordered eating. Eventually a balanced meal plan will lead to more energy, a better mood, and a healthier body.

It is also important to eat something every three to four hours. Many people think this is crazy. "If I eat breakfast, then I will be starving by lunch!" Yes, you will feel your hunger by lunch because you should. It is healthy to feel hunger every three to four hours and to respond to it. Eating every three to four hours may feel frightening in the beginning. In our society, many of us have been fooled to think, "less is more" when it comes to food. By skipping meals and going for long periods of time without food, our bodies become inefficient. Over time, our metabolism slows down making it easier to gain weight with less food. Furthermore, if you do not eat breakfast, skip lunch, and only eat at dinner, you probably will overeat, binge, or feel sick after the meal. This is your body signaling that skipping meals and not eating regularly throughout the day is not working. Listen to your body; it knows!

Learning to identify your hunger cues may be the most difficult part of the recovery process. Most individuals with eating concerns have trouble identifying and responding to hunger cues because the disordered eating behaviors have disconnected them from their physical body. Restricting, bingeing, and purging confuse the brain and make it hard for it to determine what signals to send out and when. You can retrain yourself to listen to these cues. As a baby you cried when you were hungry and stopped eating when you were full. In time, you can relearn this basic survival skill.

Changing one's relationship with food can be difficult, and a nutritionist specializing in the treatment of eating disorders can help. Those with food and weight concerns and eating disorders often feel they know everything about food, weight, and nutrition and do not find it necessary to consult with a nutritionist. In our experience, however, a one-time consult or an ongoing relationship with a nutritionist can be invaluable. You will be re-educated about healthy nutrition, learn about your unique nutritional requirements, and receive coaching on how to make small changes that will eventually lead to lasting results.

Helpful Hint:

Take a piece of paper and fold it into three sections. In the first column, write "good foods," in the middle column, write "food," and in the last column, write "bad foods." Now put down the foods you eat into the appropriate columns. How many foods are in each category? Are there any foods in the middle column, labeled "food"? Use this chart to help you identify how you think about foods and how you may label foods in black-and-white terms. Work over time to move more items into the middle "food" category. If you need help, consult a nutritionist. Remember all food provides energy, fuel, and satisfaction. Developing a healthy relationship with food takes time. When frustrated or impatient, remember the pyramid was not built in a day!

Keep Fuel in the Tank.

How often do you forget food is fuel? Instead we think of food as unwanted calories and fat grams. Diet articles tell us we will become fat if we do not carefully watch every fat gram and count every calorie consumed in a day. The mass media's message is, "Don't trust your body because it will lie to you, and only want high fat foods." No wonder we become out of touch with our natural hunger and treat our body as the enemy. The thinking of people with food and weight concerns goes one step further. The "eating disorder voice" says if less fat and calories are better, then no calories and fat grams are best. This belief leads many people to starve themselves and ignore their bodies, request for fuel.

In our society, because dieting is an obsession, you may fail to listen to your body's natural hunger cues. Unless you learn to listen and trust your body, you will be caught in a cycle of restriction (dieting) and bingeing (overeating). What is left out of many diet articles is the importance of fat to our daily food intake and the fact that calories are really a measurement used to quantify the energy or fuel we receive from the food we eat. It is important to remember we need a certain number of calories to live, and this number is unique for each individual. You would not expect your car to run without gas, so why expect your body to run without fuel? Without fuel, your automobile would be a heap of scrap metal. Without food, your body feels like a scrap heap. Be kind to your self. Fill up regularly on high-test fuel. Eat. Enjoy. You deserve it!

Helpful Hint:

Stop counting calories and fat grams. Instead, eat according to your natural hunger. A good way to figure out if you are eating for physical hunger or for emotional hunger is to use the hunger scale. The scale is from "1" (starving) to "10" (stuffed). For one day, rate your hunger before and after each time you eat a meal or a snack. The goal is to try to keep your physical hunger between "3" and "8." Many dieters go from "1" in hunger to a "10," highlighting how dieting leads to bingeing. If you have trouble with the hunger scale, you may want to work with a counselor or nutritionist. It may take time to retrain yourself to listen to your body and respond to your hunger, but it is well worth the investment.

Learn to Criticize Behaviors, Not Yourself.

A long-standing media ad used to proclaim, "You are what you eat." Of course this message was not accurate. As individuals, we are much more than what one of our actions implies. We are certainly much more than our daily caloric intake or the food groups we choose. As people, we are made up of feelings, values, and beliefs. The ad intended to get us to think about eating healthier for our body's sake. Advertisers used this sweeping statement to get us to focus on their product. The ad purposefully ignored all the other qualities that make us who we are. Its authors created a distorted message they hoped would direct our purchases.

Very frequently those with food and weight concerns judge themselves too literally on their behaviors. Although your behavior can reflect on you, you are much more than your behavior. Building your identity on your diet and exercise practices can lead you down unhealthy and self-defeating trails.

Listen to the difference between these two statements: "I don't like that I binged" versus "I don't like myself because I binged." It may sound like only a slight difference between the two, but it packs a powerful message. The first statement implies dislike of a particular behavior, and the behavior is separate from the person. It does not judge the person's entire being. The second statement, however, infers unity of the behavior and the person. It declares you to be the behavior. It overgeneralizes the behavior and casts negative judgment on you. It neglects all the other aspects of your life including your other behaviors, thoughts, and feelings. You can change behaviors, and you are more apt to do so if you associate your dissatisfaction with the behavior, not with yourself.

Helpful Hint:

Observe and record your self-criticism for a day. Do you criticize your behavior or yourself? For example, you drop a glass of milk on the kitchen floor. Do you say, "You are stupid" or "That was a stupid mistake"? When you catch yourself criticizing your whole being instead of a particular behavior, attempt to rephrase the comment so you don't personalize the action.

Use Short-Term Diversions.

In the course of your recovery you will battle the "eating disordered voice." You may know this voice well. It is the voice inside your head that shouts out all sorts of harmful thoughts and behaviors related to your food and weight concerns. This voice may tell you, "You are fat and ugly after eating a meal." It may shout at you, "Your hunger is a sign of weakness!" It may even suggest, "You are nothing unless you hold onto your eating disorder and engage in its behaviors." It is this inner unhealthy voice that drives your problem with food and weight obsession. It can be a very loud and determined voice. It can become a very familiar voice. Some people become so well acquainted with this voice, they may even name it.

For those who struggle with eating disorders or disordered eating, this unhealthy voice can assert itself over the healthy voice. The healthy voice is the voice that promotes noneating disordered thoughts and behaviors. The healthy voice may sound like many of the subtitles in this book, "You are not your dress size"; "Progress is not only measured on the scale"; and "Perfection and certainty do not exist." As you work toward recovery, it will be important to differentiate your unhealthy voice from your healthy voice. If you are uncertain as to which voice is which, a therapist can help you sort it out. At first you may find you follow the voice that directs you to engage in destructive eating and exercise behaviors. Later, you will follow your healthy voice more frequently. As you learn to differentiate between these two voices, you can begin to strategize as to how to follow your healthy voice and make it a louder, more predominant voice. Keep in mind that recovery is a gradual process toward health.

As you attempt to resist acting on the demands or directives of your unhealthy voice, use short-term diversions. Short-term diversions will serve as temporary distractions. When a small child wants to play with a dangerous item, the parent interrupts the child and provides another item or suggests an alternative. Keep in mind that much as a child might refuse to quietly relinquish playing with a dangerous item, so may your unhealthy voice get louder as protest to your healthier action. The next time you hear your disordered eating voice, try using a short-term diversion. Here are a few diversions you may find helpful:

Take a walk.
Call a friend.
Do a puzzle.
Read a book of affirmations.
Volunteer at an organization.
Play cards.
Listen to music.
Visit a museum.
See a movie.
Do something that inspires you.
Visit an elderly or sick person.
Plant a garden.
Paint your toes.
Do a craft.
Write a story.
Buy yourself some flowers.
Play a game.
Take a bath.
Be a tourist.
Go bird watching.
Sing a tune.
Write a letter.
Do an errand.
Pick apples.
Learn something new.
Fill in a few of your own: _____

Helpful Hint:

Make a list of twenty-five short-term healthy or neutral diversions you can use when you need to distract yourself from unhealthy thoughts, actions, or behaviors. Think about which ones you can use at home, school, work, or at a social gathering. Experiment with your diversions and notice which ones seem helpful and when. Remember, not all diversions are helpful 100 percent of the time. If a diversion even delays an eating disorder action, it has been useful. It has increased your tolerance to sit with a particular feeling or thought without acting destructively. Always congratulate yourself!

Progress Is Not Only Measured on the Scale.

Many treating physicians, nurses, nutritionists, and therapists, as well as those suffering from food and weight concerns and their significant others, often make the mistake of measuring progress on the scale. If the weight is up or down, progress in one's recovery is considered either poor or good. However, progress in recovery is not only measured on the scale.

While weight gain or weight loss can be a result of disordered eating, anorexia, bulimia, and binge eating are multifaceted problems. There are unique sociological, psychological, biological, familial, behavioral, and interpersonal aspects to each person's struggle. Treatment and recovery should be geared toward addressing each of these components. You can make great strides in understanding or resolving your problem with food, and it may or may not have an impact on your weight or other symptoms. One's weight may not change, or it may even go up slightly. As long as you are medically stable these shifts are to be expected and should not be seen as "poor progress." Remember eating concerns are not about weight.

Bingeing, purging, and restricting are behaviors that serve as coping mechanisms. They are behaviors that you employ to cope with life's difficulties, disappointments, traumas, fears, uncertainties, and inadequacies. You can actually be developing great insight into your behaviors but because of emotional distress, you may still need to cope by using unhealthy practices. They are what you know and what is helpful during times of distress. Your treatment should ultimately include expanding your repertoire of coping skills but in the meantime, it is important to measure your progress not solely on the scale.

Helpful Hint:

Consider either not weighing yourself or throwing away your scale. If you have the urge to step on the scale, think about what you hope to "gain" from this information. If a doctor, nurse, therapist, or nutritionist finds it necessary to weigh you, ask them not to tell you your weight. If you do weigh yourself, before getting on the scale focus on what progress you think you have made that is not about weight. Write it down, so you can remind yourself after you weigh in (e.g., "I have been able to assert myself more effectively at work"; "My laxative use is down 50 percent"; "I used a short-term diversion when I felt like bingeing").

If You Do Not Feel,
Then You Cannot Heal.

One facet of disordered eating behaviors is that they serve as one's attempt not to feel something. It could be pain, sadness, guilt, loss, love, sexuality, happiness, panic, anger, or many other countless feelings. The recovery process must include an awareness of the feelings you are attempting to avoid or numb by using your eating symptoms. You must develop the ability to identify and label feelings as you experience them. By doing so when you experience a feeling, you will have the words to label and described that feeling, as well as to more adequately determine what you may need to do to respond to it. For example, you are at the movies and you are feeling annoyed because someone is talking behind you. By recognizing and labeling your feeling, annoyance, you can determine how to respond. You can ask the offender to stop chatting. By familiarizing yourself with the variety of feelings that exist and identifying what conditions or circumstances might make you feel those different emotions, you can more easily learn how to respond when you experience one. It is similar to the way a toddler points to an object and learns its name when a willing teacher supplies it.

Many people come from families where feelings are not discussed or acknowledged. The process of becoming aware of your feelings and recognizing them can take a long time and may require a "coach" or a "teacher." However, when your recognition skills are developed, you can work on increasing your capacity to sit with those feelings, or tolerate them in order to work out a resolution and develop an alternative means of responding, or coping with them.

Feeling your feelings is a natural, essential part of the healing process. If you are going to try to heal your emotional wounds, you must first know what you are feeling. It is important to know that generally when feelings occur, they gradually intensify, peak, and then dissipate, similar to the action of an ocean wave. Feelings do not kill us, but actions aimed at suppressing them, avoiding them, denying them, or numbing them can. Let yourself connect with your feelings.

Helpful Hint:

Observe situations in which you notice you cannot identify your feelings. What are you doing at those times? How might you imagine you could feel or a friend might feel under the same circumstances? Sometimes our bodies provide us with hints to what feelings we might be experiencing. Notice any physical sensations such as muscle tightness, a sinking stomach, a lump in your throat, or a racing heart. If you find that connecting with your feelings is frightening or overwhelming, consider exploring them with a therapist. Feeling identification is a skill that can be developed with a therapist's help. Therapy is a safe place to begin to learn and use this skill.

It Is Human to Need Others.

One of the most powerful sources of energy comes from truly connecting with someone or something. Connections can fuel us during times of emptiness, tiredness, and desperation. They can feed us when we are hungry, comfort us when we are in pain, and hold us when we need protection or containment. Energy emerges when we connect with friends, family, lovers, strangers, co-workers, activities, nature, or with our spiritual beliefs. Positive feelings occur when someone or something touches our heart, reaches out and moves us, or when we simply share a single moment in time with someone. These positive feelings occur through our connections, and these connections are energizing and powerful, and can fulfill our inner needs.

It is human to need others. Frequently those with eating concerns believe it to be a shortcoming to find themselves needing others. They often believe the ideal person is self-sufficient and complete. They should be able to handle every crisis on their own, never need a ride to the garage, or accept a helping hand to plan that office party. It is as if accepting the presence of support, love, attention, or physical assistance somehow makes them less of a person. Yet it is only when we extend ourselves to others under all circumstances that we truly experience the gift in human connection.

Although seeking out others can be intimidating at first, being in the presence of others can offer us positive energy and social connection. Connection with others can be soothing, healing, motivational, nurturing, and inspirational. It decreases our isolation, loneliness, depression, self-pity, hopelessness, and despair. Reach out to others and connect; it is human.

Helpful Hint:

Be aware of how various people, activities, and experiences make you feel. Notice who or what inspires you, motivates and supports you, who you learn from, and who nurtures you. Also notice who evokes toxic reactions and negative feelings. Plan to spend more time with those people or activities which promote positive versus negative energy.

Develop Your Voice.

As young children we are often taught to "bite our tongue"—to keep comments to ourselves, particularly those remarks that are negative, mean, or hurtful. When one practices this lesson, it is considered a virtue. Its demonstration is equated with politeness, self-control, and goodness. "If you don't have anything nice to say, don't say anything at all. . . ." "Play it safe, right?" Not necessarily!

Individuals with eating concerns often take this childhood lesson far too seriously by suppressing their voice to a whisper or actually silencing it all together, losing their vocal power. It is as if the individual finds some virtue in restraining from sharing their thoughts, feelings, needs, or wishes. It can be a reflection of the sought after, over-idealized image of self-control and self-reliance. "I'm so good; I have no needs or wants." Some may play it safe, particularly when feeling vulnerable or inadequate. "If I don't say anything, there is no risk." For others it may be self-deprecation associated with a low sense of self-worth, which keeps them silent. "I won't say how I feel because I'm not important."

Refraining from using your voice leads you to disconnect from others, and more important, from yourself. When you repeatedly do not communicate with people, they will not know you. The opportunity for connection, change, or conflict resolution is lost. If you continually do not acknowledge your own inner emotions, you can end up feeling unknown to yourself, empty, deprived, and disrespected. Not using your voice to communicate can push you to seek out unhealthy behaviors as a means to express your feelings and cope with the loss of connection. Someone may binge eat when she feels intruded upon, but does not use her vocal means to protect herself, articulate her upset, or express her anger. A person experiencing anorexia may suppress her appetite when she feels overwhelmed by life tasks and has difficulty acknowledging that to herself. Starvation takes the place of asking for help.

Using your voice to express how you feel, what you need, what you wish for, or what you think is a healthy and direct way to connect with others and yourself. Instead of holding back, you are being genuine and authentic. This step will permit you to live a life of greater fulfillment. Learn to develop your voice and use it.

Helpful Hint:

Consider taking a communication workshop or an assertiveness training course at your local community college, health center, or adult education center. If this is unavailable, search out a communication or an assertiveness skills workbook and practice the techniques designed to enhance and assert your own voice.

Stay with the Day.

People with eating concerns often have trouble staying with today. They find themselves getting too far ahead worrying about the future days and events. They can be consumed with expectancy regarding making a choice, completing a task, or managing a social situation. This rumination over future concerns can often be immobilizing, compounding the obsessing and increasing stress levels. It can be very energy-consuming and can drain the person's resources.

Staying with the day means trying to keep yourself focused on what you need to concern yourself with now—concentrating on the task at hand, the meal you will eat in a moment, or the feeling you are presently experiencing. It is trying not to get too far ahead of yourself, as when you are driving and don't want to take a turn until you get to the corner. Although it is helpful to anticipate the corner, your focus must be on the present curve to prevent getting into trouble before reaching the corner or missing a delightful opportunity along the way. Staying with the day allows you to consider any unanticipated resources that may develop and that feel like a gift when they present themselves. It may be you have acquired sufficient strength to get over that hurdle you have been getting stuck on or have learned a lesson that helps you skip that old pitfall. Sometimes much more varies from one moment to another than you can predict. So when you are finding yourself immobilized by your anxieties regarding the days ahead, try to just stay with the day.

Helpful Hint:

Rate your anxiety level on a scale of one to ten. ("1" being not a care in the world, "10" being extremely anxious.) Notice at what number your anxiety level becomes overwhelming and immobilizing. When you find yourself at that point ask, "What do you need to concern yourself with right now?" Make a list of those things and try to stay with it for the day. When you find yourself drifting to other concerns, refocus on your "today" list.

Value the Instrumental, Not the Ornamental.

The human body is a miraculous thing. It has both instrumental and ornamental qualities. The instrumental aspects pertain to all the body can do, while the ornamental aspects pertain to how the body looks or appeals to our self and others. Did you know the human body has 206 bones, approximately 600 muscles, a vascular system, a reproductive system, a respiratory system, an endocrine system, an immune system, a lymphatic system, a neurological system, and many more major systems? It has numerous organs, blood vessels, veins, nerve endings, and five senses. All of this allows the body to perform many amazing and intricate functions we often take for granted. The body can walk, read and write, bear children, fight infection, respond emotionally to incoming stimuli, take in oxygen, release enzymes to digest food, and regenerate tissue. The list of all that the body can do is too expansive to print on the pages of this book.

The instrumentation of the body constantly amazes researchers, biologists, physicians, chemists, and lay people alike. It is thought to be a "marvelous machine." Yet it is absurd that, as a general rule, we tend to undervalue the body for what it does and overvalue the body for how it looks. We focus our attention on our weight, our height, and the size of our breasts, stomach, hips, and thighs. When we describe each other we emphasize our ornamental reflection to the world, as opposed to our instrumental one—who we are, what we can do, how we battle disease, support our neighbors, analyze problems, visualize space, or physically move in our bodies.

The next time you try to describe yourself or someone else consider emphasizing the instrumental aspects instead of the ornamental. Beginning to value yourself and others in this way will help you prioritize the importance of the extraordinary ways our bodies serve us, who we are on the inside, and how we contribute to those around us. It will de-emphasize the tremendous worth we attribute to our visual body image and help us to begin a new way of appreciating the body for what it can do. It will lead us away from unhealthy behaviors designed to pursue the trophy body image and lead us to a healthier, more contented relationship with our bodies.

Helpful Hint:

Draw a picture of a body. Label each body part's instrumental value and refer to it regularly (e.g., my knees provide the ability to lower my body so as I may hit a low tennis ball over the net; my hips hold up my pants; my breasts provide nourishment for my baby; my fingers type; my arms hug).

Slow and Steady Wins the Race.

Many of life's truths are learned in childhood. Remember one of Aesop's childhood fables, "The Hare and The Tortoise"? It is a story of a boasting hare that is challenged by a tortoise to a race. The hare laughingly accepts since he believes he is faster than the tortoise. After a quick start out ahead of the tortoise, the hare takes a short nap for he knows he is way ahead in the race. However, the hare oversleeps, and when he awakens the tortoise has already reached the finish line. He learns the lesson "Slow and steady wins the race."

Approach your recovery from food and weight obsessions from the tortoise's standpoint. Far too often people in treatment try to get the hare's "quick start out." They take too big a step or begin to sprint for the finish line and quickly tire. They hope this quick pace will advance them faster in their recovery. Initially, it may look like they are recovering by "leaps and bounds"; however, these people usually crash, fizzle out, lose focus, or get distracted.

Recovery is a slow and enduring process. Taking small and steady steps is the best approach. Give yourself time to stabilize or re-establish your balance after each step before going onto the next. The tortoise won the race because he focused on the finish line, not on the hare. The tortoise took one step at a time. It is important to work at your recovery at your own pace. Try not to compare yourself to others. Everyone proceeds differently and at her own rate. "Slow and steady" indeed helped the tortoise win the race. Speed is not an asset in recovery, but steadfast determination is.

Helpful Hint:

Take a realistic look at your goals and expectations as you work at your recovery. Ask yourself, "Are you shooting out like the hare and quickly needing to take breaks or are you taking small steady steps like the tortoise?" Let "slow and steady" be your personal motto.

Take One Step Outside Your Comfort Zone.

Picture a secluded tropical island. You are the only inhabitant. Your days are spent lying in a hammock under a shady palm tree. A gentle breeze blows through your hair keeping you cool. You look at the horizon, at the deep blue sea sparkling each time the sunlight reflects off a wave. It is paradise. It is comfortable.

What would happen if you spent years on the island? You would never meet anyone, make friends, fall in love, have children, laugh, or share your life. It would be safe, but it would not be living.

An eating disorder can be like the island. It gives the illusion of paradise. You hear a whisper in the wind, "If you are thin, you will be happy and life will be perfect." But preoccupation with food leads to isolation, loneliness, and unhappiness. You stop taking risks, stop loving yourself and others—you stop living. It is not paradise. It is a mirage.

Recovery happens one step outside your comfort zone. It involves stepping off the island and getting your feet wet. For instance, if you fear fatty foods, it is putting butter on your bread. If you are compelled to exercise for hours every day, it is learning to work out in moderation. If you feel anger and want to binge and purge, it is riding the feeling wave out before opening the refrigerator. If you dread conflict, it is using your voice with your partner to express your hurt feelings. Getting better involves being uncomfortable. If you wait until you feel less anxious before you take a step, you will not move along in your recovery. However, the discomfort is temporary, and pushing yourself to take small risks will ultimately lead to better living.

Helpful Hint:

Using various art supplies, make a representation of your comfort zone. What does it look like? What does it feel like? Is it large or small? Is it soft or hard? Now, expand the image to include one step outside your comfort zone. What would be in that area? Would it be family and friends? A new job? Your trigger foods? Accepting your natural weight? Share your image with a trusted friend, your physician, your nutritionist, or your therapist. Discuss how you could safely take a one small step outside your comfort zone. Remember the discomfort is temporary!

Recovery Is a Long and Winding Road.

You may believe recovery is a destination to be reached by the quickest route possible: that it is a straight line from disordered eating to normal eating. You may also believe you should be able to enter therapy and quickly progress towards recovery because your insurance company only approved eight sessions or your recovered friend was in therapy for only a few months. However, the process of recovery takes time and each person travels at a different pace. Focus less on the destinations and more on the journey. Recovery is like a long winding road through the countryside. The road takes turns and dips where least expected, but the path eventually leads you to where you need to go.

If you become impatient with your road to recovery, try to imagine yourself on a Sunday drive through the countryside. Cruising down the road, you look at the scenery, not worrying about the speed of your journey or your final destination. Similarly, your journey from food and weight obsession to health is about the scenery of self-discovery. Without self-knowledge, your path would not be rich and fruitful. The knowledge you gain along the road, like the beautiful drive along the countryside, is what feeds your soul and makes you whole. So the next time you become frustrated about the rate of your recovery, remember it is the unexpected turns in the road that will have the richest insights and lead to a long-lasting and rewarding life.

Make a collage of your road to recovery to date. Use words, magazine pictures, and your own artwork to make a visual representation of your journey. Every once in a while add to the collage. When you are feeling discouraged, look at it and see how far you have come and where you still need to go. Notice where there have been peaks and valleys. In the past, what has helped you continue along the road of recovery when you are in a valley? What happens just before a peak? Trust us—you ultimately will find your way.

Conquering the Hills and Valleys . . .

It Is Hard to Have an Appetite
When You Have a Bellyful of Feelings.

"I am just not hungry," my client said as she sat on the green office couch. She had finished an eating disorders inpatient treatment program a month ago. Crying, she said she did not know why she did not have an appetite.

After talking about what was happening this week, it became clear she was struggling with many mixed emotions. Scared, angry, sad, and lonely were a few. The transition from the hospital to home had been difficult. She realized the hospital stay was not a cure. It did help, but sitting with different feelings made following the meal plan troublesome. Together we worked to help her understand how these feelings may lead her to skip meals and not feel hungry. I gently said, "It is hard to have an appetite when you have a bellyful of feelings." Through the tears, she smiled. "That's it!"

In our society, women are taught to be nice, lady-like, and be "made of sugar and spice." The problem with this societal message is that it does not allow us to be human and express anger, resentment, sadness, frustration, and fear. As an attempt to live up to being a "nice, little girl," we use food to stuff our feelings or redirect them against ourselves. How many of us find it easier to be angry at ourselves for not losing weight or not working out, than to be angry at a friend or a partner for hurtful words or actions?

Part of the challenge of recovery is to figure out when you are emotionally full and how you can express those emotions safely. Healthy ways of expression include talking to a trusted friend or a therapist, writing in a journal, walking in a beautiful place, crying, or taking time to let the feeling pass. Unhealthy ways include starving, bingeing, purging, compulsive exercising, or hurting oneself.

As part of the recovery process, you need to figure out when you are physically full from food as opposed to emotionally full from feelings. If you have trouble distinguishing between the two, then it may be helpful to work with a nutritionist who specializes in eating concerns and eating disorders. This professional can evaluate your current eating habits in a nonjudgmental way, help you determine what your unique nutritional needs are, and work with you to change your unhealthy behaviors. You can learn to recognize your physical hunger and how to respond to it nutritionally. Once this is mastered, you can work to recognize your emotional hunger and how to respond to it safely.

So the next time you feel like skipping a meal or engaging in unhealthy eating practices, make sure you ask yourself the following questions: "Am I emotionally full or physically full?" "What am I feeling?" Once you have the answers, you can respond to the bellyful of feelings in a healthy way.

Helpful Hint:

The next time you have a bellyful of feelings, draw a picture of your stomach with all the feelings inside. Be creative. Use magazine pictures and words, crayons, paint, clay, and fabric. You may be surprised at what your picture or sculpture looks like and how it helps relieve your emotional fullness.

Fear Not Your Feelings;
Every Feeling Has a Special Gift.

There is a range of feelings one can experience, but some seem or are experienced as more pleasurable than others. If we could choose our feelings, one might pick falling in love over feeling depressed, feeling elated over feeling angry, or feeling proud over feeling anxious. Some feelings indeed are easier to live with or to sit with. Consider, however, that each feeling has a special gift. Some feelings give us pleasure, like feelings of love, happiness, pride, and elation. Others are unpleasant, like the pain of a divorce, anxiety over a new job, or grief from the loss of a significant other. However, all emotions are valuable and behold their own special gift.

Feelings actually provide us with information about our lives. Without them we might miss important information not found through other cues. Depression or despair can be a sign something is not right for us. It provides us with the gift of opportunity for change. We usually have more motivation or drive to make a change or try something new when we feel despair. Most people who have recovered from eating and body image concerns first felt their pain and despair before braving change and eventual recovery. They were motivated by their pain to take risks, and explore options.

When we feel anger we often feel power to assert ourselves and effect change. Anger's gift is power. We generally feel most entitled and empowered when we feel angry. Have you ever confronted someone when you were angry? Did you notice how much power you felt? Way to go anger!

Guilt is a very central feeling for those who suffer from eating concerns. Guilt's special gift is responsibility. When one feels guilt, one has to explore and determine where responsibility lies and where boundaries may need to be drawn. One usually will ask questions about accountability. Feeling guilt helps you to focus on your answerability regarding your actions.

Feelings come and feelings go. They come in all sorts of comfort and pleasure levels, and each serves an important purpose. They connect us to reality and give us very useful information. Like a security system in a building, feelings can tell us when we are being intruded upon, on fire, under siege, in great working order, or on the verge of some significant external or internal event. Do not fear your feelings, but use them to give you information about your life.

Helpful Hint:

Identify feelings you find difficult to sit with or experience. Attempt to see their special gift by asking yourself what information the feelings provide about your life or what action they encourage you to take. Make a list of each of these feelings and their gifts to remind you of their value. For example: When I feel fear, as I am approached by a growling animal, I am usually encouraged to run, back off, or proceed with caution. Fear's hidden gift is to provide awareness of danger.

It Is Not Selfish to Take Care of Yourself.

It is essential to take care of yourself! Consider your personal bank account. Your account generally has a cash balance or range within which you feel comfortable. As long as you maintain that minimum balance, you feel financially secure and settled. However, if you are constantly drawing on your balance, at some point you will overdraw and become financially unstable. As you acquire debt and bounce checks, it just gets more and more overwhelming. It is important for you to make regular deposits to handle the withdrawals. You must replenish the funds, or suffer the consequences of overdrawing.

Think of yourself as a bank account. Let's call it a self-care account. Very often we have demands put upon us for our money, our time, our service, or our emotional support. If we only give to others or tend only to others' needs, without making any type of deposit into our self-care account, we come up short, overdrawn, exhausted, and wiped out. Taking care of ourselves is essential to running a balanced and fulfilling life. We need to find ways in which we can give to ourselves so we can replenish for the demands of others and life's typical daily stress. Taking care of yourself is a responsibility, not a selfish act.

Helpful Hint:

Make a list of twenty things you can do to give to yourself. Include a range of quick pick-me-ups to more time-consuming and involved self-care acts. Keep the list close at hand and refer to it often, particularly when your account balance is low. Some ideas are: play with your cat, dog, or kids; read a good book; get a massage; learn to dance; give someone a hug; or buy yourself a small gift that is truly frivolous. Make deposits regularly!

Strive to Be Average.

In our achievement-oriented society, we often feel pressured to be the best. Get the best job. Make the most money. Buy the biggest house. For some, the pursuit of perfection becomes a life goal. As a result, this unattainable objective leaves us feeling bad about ourselves. Achievements are minimized and self-criticism creeps in. When you should be rejoicing that you were brave enough to take a risk, you are renouncing yourself for missing the mark.

What is the cost of this quest? For the student studying night and day to get straight A's, it is missing out on the social aspects of school. For the businessperson who is a workaholic, it is the time she could have spent at her son's baseball game. For the housewife who spends many hours a day at the gym trying to achieve physical perfection, it is the lost opportunity to meet friends, play with her kids, or pursue her dreams. All in all the cost can be great.

Perfectionism comes in many forms. Some clients are searching for the ideal body. Others are trying to be the perfect daughter, wife, or mother. Some have a more subtle form of perfectionism—the search to be a perfect human who has the "right" feelings in each life situation. To never lose their temper, never cry, never feel scared or lonely. To be robotic in their emotional and physical lives.

Life is messy. Human nature is imperfect. It is what makes us interesting and unique. Our flaws, while at times frustrating, can endear us to others. Take the example of a friend who is always late for social gatherings. Initially, this may annoy you. Later in your relationship, you realize the cause of her tardiness was her wonderful gift of living in the moment. Suddenly this flaw became a strength—just part of who she is as a person.

What would it be like to strive to be average? To replace the thought you had to be the number one employee, daughter, athlete, student, or wife with the idea that being okay, at each, was enough. You could focus on enjoying the act of living instead of the act of achieving. In the beginning, this may feel like giving up or failing. But with time and practice, the pursuit of being average can be freeing. You can have fun. Enjoy the task at hand. Laugh when you mess up. Striving to be average can be the best thing you have ever done!

Helpful Hint:

Imagine you wake up one morning with the desire to be average. Envision what your life would be like. Write a short story, a journal entry, or a play about your experience. Focus on what you would gain. Re-read this story when you need a reminder of the benefits striving to be average can bring.

Norman Rockwell Does Not Live Here Anymore.

Norman Rockwell was a painter who painted pictures of American life. The family members were all smiling as they sat around the holiday dinner table, eagerly awaiting a perfect meal with wonderful conversation. In the pictures, it looked like the holiday of a lifetime.

Is that how it is at your house? For most, the answer is no. More often than not, holidays include financial and family stress. Conflicts are commonplace, and perfection does not exist. No, Norman Rockwell does not live here anymore.

Holidays can be one of the most difficult times for people struggling with eating concerns. Thanksgiving, Christmas, Chanukah, and New Year's all center on big, elaborate meals and high expectations. Bingeing on food is an acceptable holiday pastime. The season is filled with parties, sweets, and drinks to make you merry. If you are food and weight obsessed, the holidays can be quite overwhelming. What you hope will be a perfect day is just another day and another meal with the same imperfect family sitting at the table.

So how can you manage your anxiety around the holiday season? First of all, lower your expectations. There is no perfect Christmas, New Year's, or Chanukah celebration. Accept it and strive to have an enjoyable, average holiday. Second, plan for the day. If a big meal is overwhelming for you, work with your nutritionist, therapist, and/or family members to help make the food more manageable. It is best to stick to the same meal plan you follow on other days. Do not skip breakfast and lunch. It is a setup for a binge. Instead, eat your regular meals and snacks, making the main holiday meal one of them. Ask the person serving the meal if they can schedule the dinner around lunch or dinnertime so it does not throw off your eating schedule. Ask for safe foods to be served as part of the meal. Safe foods are foods that are not going to trigger bingeing, purging, or restricting. Next, ask for support. Talk with the members of your support system. These may include a parent, a favorite aunt or uncle, or a friend. Tell them, in advance, how they can help and what might be hard about the day. Set up regular holiday check-in times in case you need support. Lastly, develop a new holiday ritual to take the sole focus off the meal. Some rituals include playing board games after dinner, taking a family walk to check out the holiday lights, or writing or telling a story about what each member of the family is thankful for this year. Be creative and ask for input from others when deciding on your new family ritual.

So even though Mr. Rockwell is not showing up at your house this year, you can enjoy the holidays. Focus on what is really important—your family and friends, your health, and your recovery. You may just enjoy the holidays after all.

Helpful Hint:

Set up an appointment with your parents or loved ones to discuss the holiday a few weeks before the event. If you need support, this meeting can happen in your therapist's or nutritionist's office. At this meeting, discuss what structure might help you on that day, what safe foods can be served, and what supports you might want to put in place. Allow your loved ones to talk about what they are willing to compromise on and what they feel they need to keep to make the holidays feel special to them. Together decide on a non-food-related ritual to start. Who knows, it could take off and be used for generations to come.

What Is Done Is Done!

How often do you find yourself saying, "I should have said this . . ." or "What if I said that . . ."? This type of questioning often leads to obsessive thinking. When we obsess about the past, we are trying to control the uncontrollable. What you can control are your thoughts and actions in the present. What is done is done!

Jane, a 43-year-old compulsive overeater, came into her weekly therapy session upset. She had binged the night before and was very anxious and depressed. Jane had not binged in 6 months and felt as if she had blown her recovery. She knew her binge was triggered by a disagreement with her mother. She had spent the hours since their fight asking "what if" questions and worrying about what she might have done differently. Jane even went so far as to revisit all of her disagreements with her mother in the past.

What Jane had not realized is that what she was worrying about was no longer in her control. She had fought with her mom and could not change how they interacted last night. No matter how much she revisited their argument, she could not change it. However, in her therapy session, she learned she could choose to act differently with her mother in future discussions. Her small slip was a sign she needed to continue to work on asserting herself with her family. Once Jane could let go of her obsessive thoughts, she could use her energy more constructively to learn how to be more assertive. She realized what was done, was done.

In recovery, it is important to learn to let go of the past and concentrate on the present moment. Be mindful of where you are, how you feel, and what you think in the moment. Remind yourself that no one is perfect. If you are uncomfortable with something you have said or done, learn from that experience. By looking at what was done, learning from it, asserting yourself, and letting it go, you will feel free—and freedom can feel weightless regardless of the numbers on the scale.

Helpful Hint:

If you find yourself constantly thinking about something you did or said, practice "thought stopping." Thought stopping is a behavioral technique to help with obsessive thoughts. Each time the troublesome thought occurs, you say "stop" out loud. By giving yourself this verbal cue, you are training yourself to stop the obsessing and focus on the present moment. Eventually, you will train yourself to stop the thought without the verbal cue. By practicing this technique you will learn to let go and focus on the present. Be patient with yourself. It takes a while to break any habit.

Quiet Your Mind.

At one point during the writing of this book, we went to Vermont for a "writing retreat" to quiet our minds. It was a retreat I felt I desperately needed. In order to write, I needed to remove myself from the activities of my daily life with my children, my husband, my work, my civic and community interests, my friends, and my extended family. I find all these activities extremely satisfying; however, at times they can make it difficult to clear my head or organize my thoughts for writing. Quieting your mind is an essential practice in creating, rejuvenating, growing, and discovering. It is the idea of attempting to periodically remove yourself from life's distractions, both literally and figuratively, so you can quiet your mind. You'll be amazed at the results!

Quieting your mind is a skill, a process that takes practice and time to acquire. Although simply stated, quieting your mind requires physically removing yourself from all distractions and "clearing your head." It is allowing your thoughts and feelings to come and go without you controlling them. This is not a simple process, but it is well worth the time and energy to learn.

Quieting your mind can be practiced in a number of ways through relaxation, meditation, yoga, or prayer. It involves the focused concentration of temporarily clearing your mind of your worries, responsibilities, fears, and obsessions, and becoming mindful of just being present to yourself at that particular moment. It is what many refer to as "staying in the here and now," "being present to yourself," or "being mindful." Quieting your mind can be practiced almost at any time or any place. You can be seated or not. It can be as quick as several seconds, or practiced for more extended periods of time. It is important to know that at first you may feel unsure and tentative. You may question whether you are doing it right or you may become easily frustrated by experiencing numerous thought intrusions. These reactions are typical for beginners learning to acquire this skill. Stick with it. In time it will become easier and more comfortable. You may even reap immense rewards.

Helpful Hint:

Locate a meditation center or yoga studio in your area and take an introductory course. If you do not live in a community with such access, buy an audio or videotape in the self-help section at a bookstore or video store. Beginners often need the guidance of an instructor to learn this skill. Once you have acquired some of the basics, consider taking a minute or two each morning or evening to tune in to the sounds and sights of the day. This small practice will lead to increased mindfulness.

Who Says You "Should"?

I should eat only "good" foods. I shouldn't have eaten that cookie. I should always be happy. I should . . . I should . . . I should . . . Who says? Where does that voice come from? Do you listen, or do you tell it to be quiet?

All of us experience what is called self-talk. Self-talk is a running dialogue we have with ourselves throughout the day. Self-talk is a voice we sometimes hear loudly and sometimes do not notice at all. It resembles a mental audiotape filled with messages received throughout our lifetime. Some of the messages are positive such as, "say thank you after someone opens the door for you," and some are negative such as, "you should never be wrong." We get into trouble when the tapes we hear are more destructive than supportive.

"Should" statements often get us into trouble by setting up unrealistic expectations of perfection. When we do not meet those expectations, we feel like failures. However, we are asking ourselves to do the impossible, to be perfect. This is why we recommend you start listening to all the "should" statements in your self-talk. When you start hearing yourself say "should," try to stop and ask yourself "who says?" Think about the messages you are feeding yourself and where they may have originated. Are they nurturing messages to help you in your recovery, such as you should eat every three to four hours, or hurtful tapes learned in childhood, such as you should not get angry. We all have tapes in our heads from our youth, but as adults we can choose to listen to them or to create new ones with healthier, kinder thoughts.

How do you do this? It takes time, practice, and some coaching. It starts by noticing your self-talk, then working to turn the unhealthy messages into healthy ones. Often a therapist or support group can help with this skill. For years you have been quietly reinforcing all the "should" statements, so it takes time and support to challenge them. Be patient.

Picture yourself painting a dark blue room white. As your paintbrush goes over the blue paint, a thin layer of white paint is left behind. You still see the blue paint and in some areas the dark color is still quite noticeable. You go back and paint the walls with a second coat. This time the white areas fill in and only a little blue is showing. By the third coat, you would never be able to guess the original color of the room. This is similar to how you change your unhealthy messages. You have a dark layer of "shoulds," and you are painting your mind over with white, healthier messages. It takes time and energy and feels exhausting at times. But eventually, the old paint disappears, and the new paint shines brightly, lighting up the room.

Helpful Hint:

Next time you hear yourself saying "should" statements, do not assume they are rules to live by. Instead, stop and question them. Write the statements down in a journal and challenge them. What supports that belief? What questions that belief? Decide for yourself what you should or should not do. There is no one right answer; there is just your answer. Be true to yourself. Who says you "should" anyway?

Take Compliments Gracefully.

"I never take a compliment when someone gives me one," Lisa declared. When asked why, she retorted that she felt she "did not deserve them." Individuals with eating and body image concerns often have a very low sense of self-worth and self-esteem. They frequently don't see themselves as others do. They can distort their perceptions of their merits, their appearance, and their uniquely treasured personal qualities. These misperceptions can occur for numerous reasons that need to be explored in greater detail as one travels along the road toward recovery.

Learn to take compliments. It is a good habit, and it promotes self-esteem, increases a sense of self-worth, and often helps us be in touch with our innate skills and strengths. Listen to a compliment (that's not fishing for one), instead of deflecting it, tossing it aside, or rejecting it altogether. Consider the impact of long-term rejection of all positive feedback. Constant negativity generates poor self-esteem, low self-worth, depression, hopelessness, helplessness, and inertia. When you don't take compliments or when you reject them, you put up a screen. That screen allows only negative feedback to penetrate, setting you up for self-esteem deficits, which can fuel eating problems, trigger poor self-care, or activate behaviors designed to over-compensate for perceived shortcomings.

Listen for compliments, record them, count them, embrace them, and thank those who give them to you. They can be a gift to behold and treasure. Take compliments: it is recommended daily.

Helpful Hint:

Say "thank you" when you are paid a compliment. Don't minimize it, devalue it, or dismiss it. Let yourself hear it, register it consciously, and call upon it when your confidence needs a boost.

Laugh at Yourself.

One of the greatest gifts we have as humans is our ability to laugh. Laughter brings joy into our lives. It can create intimacy. Think about the last time you shared a joke with someone. In that moment, did you feel closer? Laughter can also help us defend ourselves from painful feelings until we are ready to cope with them. The saying "laugh until you cry" comes from the idea that laughter can help until you are able to feel the pain, cry, and get over it. Research studies have proven laughter lowers stress levels.

If you are like many people with food and weight concerns, you may find it hard to let go and have fun. Those who grew up in a house with alcoholism, trauma, or chaos often did not learn how to play. They were too busy surviving. If you are one of those people, then you may need to actively learn the skills involved in laughing and being playful in life.

When you feel depressed or when your problems with food and weight preoccupation become overwhelming, try to find something to laugh about. This is not to say your struggle with food is funny. It is not. But at times, the best treatment is to step outside your problem and see the funny side of life.

Helpful Hint:

Add laughter to your life. Laugh with a friend, a lover, a pet, or a stranger. Watch a funny movie, television show, or stand-up comedy routine. Just laugh. It can make you feel ten times lighter.

Go with Your Grain.

There is an old saying that goes like this, "Don't go against your grain for personal gain." It likely originated when a wood craftsman noticed the beauty that emerged as he labored over a piece of wood. He noticed if he sanded and stained the wood in the direction of the wood's natural grain, it exposed the wood's innate beauty. But when he worked the wood against its natural grain, it splintered and cracked.

Many people with eating and weight concerns work against their own grain. They splinter, crack, and destroy themselves emotionally and physically. Rather than accepting the natural beauty of their unique body type, they try to go against their grain, employing behaviors and practices which only damage their bodies. However, significant and severe medical consequences to your body can result from chronic dieting, vomiting, abusing laxatives, taking diuretics, using diet pills, compulsively over-eating, and excessively exercising. When we strive to work our bodies against our natural genetic "set-point," we may experience electrolyte and hormonal imbalances, bone and muscle loss, ruptured esophagus, tooth decay, irregular heart rates, hypertension, intestinal and stomach problems, depression, and social isolation. This is only a partial list of complications. Engaging in anorexic, bulimic, and binge-eating behaviors carries many more risks than can be listed here.

Each person has a natural set-point weight range. This is the weight range their body was genetically predetermined to function and operate best within. It is not an exact number, but a range of weight. It is unique for every individual. It is like the unique grain in a piece of wood. The set-point weight range is the weight range your body will fight to maintain and that will permit most body functions to be carried out properly and regularly. Accepting your natural set-point range will help you achieve optimum health and inner peace. Your physician or nutritionist can help you determine what your set-point range is. It is often hard to hear what it is, as sometimes it may not be the range we wish for; however, if you try to work against it, you will suffer consequences medically, physically, emotionally, and socially.

Working against yourself, ignoring your needs, sabotaging your success, not following your heart, or not accepting your set-point weight range are all examples of going against your grain. Doing so, little by little, chips away at you until you disappear or are destroyed. Go with your grain, follow your heart, attend to your needs, accept your set-point, and trust your gut feelings. Watch your unique beauty emerge!

Helpful Hint:

Get a piece of wood and sandpaper from your local hardware store. Notice the wood's grain and begin to sand it in the opposite direction. Notice the resistance and the chipping that occurs. Now sand your wood in the direction of its grain. Notice the increased ease in which the task can be done, the intensity of the grain's shine, and the feel of the wood. No chips, no splinters, no rough edges. The wood's unique beauty shines. Use this image to help you in your recovery.

Feeling and Acting in Beautiful Ways Showcases Your Beauty.

Have you ever observed a bride on her wedding day, a child readying herself for a special religious ceremony, a preschooler singing her ABC's, a soccer player saving a shot on goal, a graduate walking down the processional aisle, or a new grandparent holding their hour-old grandchild? The excitement generated over these momentous occasions exudes beauty. These moments are not about how one looks at the prescribed time of glory, but how one feels and what one has achieved. It is at moments like these we can see through and past superficial media images of beauty and know that true beauty comes from within and in many forms. It is not about what one looks like on the outside, but about how one lives and embraces one's life.

Beauty does not reveal itself in a lipstick or in cosmetic reconstructive surgery, but in the manner one connects and gives to others. It is not about perfection, success, fame, or fortune. Beauty is seen in the way one makes commitments to friends, lovers, or causes. It is the way one respects and participates in traditions or religious rituals. It is the pride one feels when one accomplishes a task of any scale. Or the ability to make someone laugh, console their pain, or feel understood. It is the unique manner in which one loves, plays, allows oneself to be vulnerable, demonstrates one's imperfections, or simply participates and emotes in the world that showcases one's beauty. You are uniquely beautiful. Let others see and feel it.

> ## Helpful Hint:
>
> Write down three friends and family members and list the qualities about them which attracted you to them. Notice how many of those traits are physical and ornamental versus how many are related to the expression of beauty which is showcased as they live their lives.

Beware of the "Crunch"!

We all have a crunch time in our lives. Crunch time is a term, that I first became aware of in college. It was that time in the semester in which you felt "in a crunch" to produce term papers, design projects, deliver speeches, finish the reading, study for tests, or complete research. Inevitably it would feel like everyone wanted everything all at once, and you felt "in a crunch" to produce massive amounts of work in a condensed period of time. Crunch time is a universal experience for all of us. It stretches across all developmental phases of life from at least adolescence to late adulthood; however, those with eating concerns may be particularly vulnerable to its stress. Adolescents frequently report feeling the crunch when applying to college, when they need to fill out applications, write essays, obtain letters of recommendation, visit colleges, and go on interviews—all the while, maintaining their daily schedules and extracurricular activities. College students, as I mentioned above, typically feel it at midterms and finals. Young adults can feel the crunch in their first job, when looking for a life partner, or when returning to a class reunion. While mid-life adults may feel it during hectic times of life, as when juggling holiday festivities, sometimes with more than one family to keep in mind, when driving kids to activities, or when preparing for a work presentation just before their daughters' end of the year dance recitals. Late-life adults may experience the crunch time when they feel up against the clock to complete life goals, realize dreams, or resolve long-standing issues.

Being cognizant of your personal crunch times can be very helpful. It can allow you to keep your perspective regarding the inevitable stress you may feel and accept it as a normal reaction to what you are experiencing. It can allow you to be proactive about coping with stress instead of being reactive to it

The symptoms of eating disorders are often a means to cope with stressful experiences. Obsessive calorie counting or over-exercising can distract you from the feelings provoked by the numerous tasks at hand. Abusing laxatives can be an attempt to neutralize feelings of being out of control during hectic times. Compulsively overeating can numb or stuff down the myriad of feelings you find intolerable during the crunch time. Being aware when you are heading into a stressful period of your life can help you to be prepared to utilize healthier coping strategies to combat expected cyclical stressors because you are prepared for the onslaught of stress that you know comes with the "crunch." It allows you to be proactive to your choice of coping style rather than reactive, which can often lead to impulsive and frequently unhealthy ways of managing the stress. Beware of the "crunch"!

Helpful Hint:

Look back over a year's period of time and jot down the activities and demands placed on you typically during the months of the year. Some examples are planning an annual cookout, adjusting to the start of a new school year, scheduling holiday celebrations, mourning the anniversary of a loved one's death, preparing for vacation, or waiting for expected news. Create a strategy list of healthy approaches to the crunch time, like ensuring proper rest and nutrition, accepting offers of help, taking medication as directed, avoiding extra activities, or taking on additional commitments. Develop strategies to cope with the crunch time while you are in it, like taking it a task at a time, taking breaks to laugh, connecting with others, relaxing, compromising, reassessing your expectations, and making adjustments if necessary.

Life Is Too Short to Wear Uncomfortable Shoes!

Would you ever buy a pair of shoes that were two sizes too small in the hopes someday your feet would shrink and they would fit? Probably not! It would be absurd. So why is it not absurd when women have the same thought about clothes?

It is a common for individuals struggling with eating concerns to own an expandable wardrobe. This is a closet full of clothes, which range in size from "fat" clothes to "thin" clothes, to every size in between. Some people could open up a consignment shop with all the apparel in their closet that does not currently fit them. The theory behind the expandable wardrobe is that if you buy an outfit two sizes too small, then you will be motivated to lose weight. Has this ever worked? The truth is 95 percent of all diets fail. Therefore, the idea that the latest fad diet will suddenly be successful because you have clothes that do not fit is ridiculous. Yet, as a society we buy into this belief daily and fill our closets with never-to-be-worn motivational attire.

It is almost impossible to gain and maintain body confidence when wearing clothes that are not fitted properly. A dress, skirt, or blouse that is too small for our physical bodies will make us feel too big. In reality we are not too big, the clothes are too small. Tight pants are not medically healthy and can be emotionally abusive. Furthermore, the physical discomfort fuels unhealthy thinking. The fact that the clothes are not the right size is lost and replaced with the thought, "If I am not a size 6, 12, or 18 . . . then I must be fat." This in turn can lead to more dieting, bingeing, restricting, and symptomatic behaviors. Clothes that are too small make us crabby, uncomfortable, discouraged, and depressed. All around, it is a recipe for unhappiness.

While the idea of putting away or giving away your "thin" clothes and buying only clothes that fit sounds easy, the truth of the matter is, it can be an emotionally difficult process. Your "thin" wardrobe represents all the hopes and dreams you have connected with losing weight. In letting go of these clothes, you are symbolically letting go of the myth that thinness equals happiness. It is often a myth that dies hard. The act of giving these clothes away is the act of accepting your genetics and accepting your body as is for now. The process can make one sad, angry, and frustrated. It may feel like failing. But you are winning, because it is an important step toward body acceptance and full recovery.

So give up your expandable wardrobe. Throw them out or donate them. Acknowledge the mixed feelings that go along with saying goodbye to your "thin" clothes. Feel the sadness, the anger, and the grief. Buy clothes in the size you are today. Purchase shirts, pants, skirts, and blouses that are comfortable. Buy garments made of fabrics that feel good against your skin. Celebrate your body size. After all, life is too short to wear uncomfortable shoes.

Helpful Hint:

Pack up your "thin" clothes and give them away to your favorite charity. It will make you and your accountant happy!

Coffee, Croissants, and Conflict.

All relationships have a certain amount of conflict. In general, individuals with food and weight concerns are conflict avoidant. Often the belief is, if I have a fight with someone, that person will no longer like me. Many grew up in a family where disagreements were taboo, avoided at all costs, or downright physically dangerous. Without parents who can model how to effectively fight, a child does not learn this important skill. Conflict resolution is a skill that leads to greater self-confidence and healthier relationships. So why coffee, croissants, and conflict? Because we believe everyone needs to make time for conflict. We take time out of our day for a cup of coffee, when healthy, for food and drink, but often we do not make time for conflict.

What happens when disagreements are avoided? The result is often anger at oneself or others that does not get expressed and/or resolved. Many women stuff down the anger with food or drink or obsess about a recent incident instead of dealing with the problem directly. Others talk to everyone but the person they are frustrated with. This just leads to more frustration, agitation, and assumptions. The problem still exists and often the person at whom you are angry still has no idea you have feelings about it or does not understand what made you upset.

So it is important to learn to fight in a fair and assertive way. If you are someone who is passive, it will take time and practice to learn how to effectively express your feelings and resolve conflicts. If you are someone who is aggressive and is likely to lash out at someone, you also need to learn to slow down and practice healthy conflict resolution skills. The good news is, it can be learned. When fighting is done well, both individuals feel better about themselves and their relationship. So take the time to try your hand at healthy conflict.

Helpful Hint:

Set aside a time to discuss conflicts with your partner, friend, loved one, or roommate. Just as you would schedule a meeting to discuss house finances or household chores that need to be done, you need to make time to discuss differences. If you find that this time is turning into a war zone, you may consider taking a conflict resolution course or going to a counselor to learn how to communicate better when conflict is present.

Get Off the Sidelines and Get into the Ball Game.

"If I lost weight I would . . . start dating, find a new job, join a gym . . ." How many times have you started a sentence with that phrase? Are you waiting to get active and get in the ball game of life once you hit a certain number on the scale? If you are someone who has stopped living until the diet works, you need to keep in mind that 95 percent of diets fail. So why wait?

The dieter's myth says that at my "ideal weight" I will not be anxious trying a new activity, making a new friend, or meeting a special someone. It will become miraculously easy. This belief is reinforced by advertisements that tell us that losing weight will boost our confidence, improve our social life, and make us happy. The truth is that in the long run, the size of our body or the numbers on the scale will not make life easier. As with anything new, the initial experience may be anxiety-provoking. (Remember one step outside your comfort zone.) But the discomfort will be temporary. It will pass. The anxiety will lessen. Once it does, the payoffs are big. An active lifestyle has been proven to reduce depression, anxiety, and stress as well as increase your life expectancy. Your self-confidence will improve along with your body confidence.

So go to the beach. Wear a bathing suit. Date. Start yoga. Learn to knit. Join a theater group or a book club. Go skiing in the winter and sailing in the summer. Find your passion. Whatever it is, pursue it, and get into the ball game!

Helpful Hint:

Close your eyes and imagine what your life would be like at your ideal weight. What clothes would you wear? How would you feel in your body? Who would be in your life? Now imagine doing all the same things at your current weight. What would it be like now? Examine your reasons for putting activities and relationships on hold. In the next week, try at least one thing you have been putting off until you reach your ideal weight. Have fun!

Before Growth, One Generally Experiences a Lull.

Have you hit a plateau? Do you feel like your work on recovery has come to a standstill or is not progressing? Well do not be so quick to question yourself, your recovery process, your therapist, your doctor, or anyone else. Before growth, one often experiences a lull or a quieting of activity. It can appear as if nothing is happening although there may be considerable progress going on.

Consider one of the many examples in nature. In the Northeast, the fall season leaves us with bare trees and barren grounds for the winter, which appears to be an inactive season. However, when the spring season erupts with blossoms, buds, flowers, and new growth, it reminds us that although we did not perceive much activity, plenty was occurring.

At times outward signs of movement or progress may not be observable to others or yourself, but stick with it. Often there is a quieting of self, a collecting of one's thoughts, or a stabilizing period just after a new skill is developed or before a new insight emerges. It is as if we are storing up energy for the next phase of growth. Be patient with the quiet inactive times; there may be a blossom about to emerge into full bloom!

Helpful Hint:

During a quiet time in your recovery process look back at your path to date. Notice your journey and recall important times, incidences, insights, and changes. Do you notice an ebb and flow pattern? Enjoy the blossoms, and take stock in the mountains you have climbed. For those who find this difficult, talk with your therapist or use a support group to help you identify the significant growth shoots and buds in your recovery.

You Can't Buy Something from an Empty Store.

We often look for emotional support from people who cannot give it to us. We look for characteristics and traits in our parents, our partners, and our friends which are not in their inventory. We may want an emotional connection with a parent who does not know how to show his or her feelings. We may crave mature romantic love from a person who is not capable of loving us this way. We may search for understanding from people who can only connect on a superficial level. Why do we continue to search for love, nurturing, and support where we have not found it?

A perfect example of this phenomenon is a story told to us by Susie, a 35-year-old woman recovering from binge-eating disorder. Susie came into a session crying. She had just learned that a close relative of her husband's had suddenly died of cancer. She was devastated by the loss and had called her mother to let her know about the funeral arrangements and get comfort in her grief. "Can you believe her first words were 'Dad and I can't make it to the funeral because I have a hair appointment.' " Clearly, Susie was hurt and angered by her mom's insensitive response.

Susie, like many of us, was shopping in an empty store. Imagine going to the convenience store for a loaf of bread. Picture yourself walking into the store and finding there was nothing on the shelves. The store was empty. Ask the storeowner for a loaf of bread and envision the request falling on deaf ears. Imagine this scenario playing itself out over and over. No matter how often you ask or how much you wish the store carried the bread, it does not. Using this imagery, Susie discovered she had two choices. She could go to a different store, or she could go without bread.

In time, Susie realized that nurturing and validating feelings was not her mom's strong suit. Looking for something her mom could not give her was like shopping in an empty store. She came to realize that other people in her life could fulfill this role, and in tough times, she turned to them for comfort. Once Susie realized her mom was not withholding love, but simply was giving what she had to give, she became more amused by her mom's shortcomings and less hurt by them.

In recovery, it is important to take an inventory of all the things the important people in your life can and cannot give you. It is also vital to distinguish what is your responsibility to work on versus what is someone else's issue. Once you have taken inventory, you must realize that in certain circumstances, it may be healthier to not ask for something a person cannot give. So if you find yourself repeatedly shopping in an empty store, stop and ask yourself why. It may be time to find a new place to shop.

Helpful Hint:

Take inventory in the stores you shop in regularly. For instance, write a list of "in stock" and "out of stock" items for each person in your life. Be realistic about the inventory, and recognize the only one who can stock the shelves is the storeowner.

Husband:	In stock	Out of stock
	Caring	Financial savvy
	Supportive	Neatness
	Patient	
	Fun	

Practice, Practice, Practice.

There is a learning theory that states people tend to learn skills in steps. Once the skill is acquired, they will experience occasional lapses in the performance of that skill until it is completely mastered. For example, think of a young child learning to ride a bicycle. At first the child will be taught the steps of riding a bicycle such as: steering the bicycle, peddling the pedals, braking, or balancing herself on the bicycle. The child at some point will string these steps together in the proper sequence and acquire the ability to ride a bicycle. However, it is quite natural for a child to one day have the skill to ride a bicycle, and on the next day not be able to put the sequence together successfully. The child will have lapses in her acquisition of a skill until she masters it. Mastering happens when a skill is internalized as a part of oneself. This develops through practice and repetition. All skills are learned this way.

In the recovery process, there are many new skills to learn. One must learn to identify feelings, assert and use one's voice, sit with difficult feelings, respond to needs, communicate directly, and expand one's repertoire of coping skills. Be patient and understanding with yourself. Treat yourself as if you were a young child learning to ride a bicycle for the first time. Try to remember your new skills may first appear in pieces or parts. Expect lapses until the skills are mastered. Remember to practice, practice, practice and to be kind to yourself as you work on the acquisition. Nurture yourself when frustration emerges as lapses occur, and clap for yourself when you get it right!

Helpful Hint:

Pick one recovery skill you are trying to develop. Some suggestions include learning to eat every 3 to 4 hours, sitting with the feeling of a full stomach, or saying "no" to requests when you feel you have too much to do. Break the skill down into steps. Talk with a friend, therapist, sponsor, or coach if you are having difficulty doing this. Give yourself support and encouragement, and the reassurance that through practice, the skill can be acquired.

Continuing
the Journey . . .

Slips Don't Always Lead to Slides.

As a neophyte therapist, I was paired up with a more experienced one to run a recovery group in a community mental health center. My co-therapist was a very warm, open, and supportive man, who worked for many years in the substance abuse field. He often used to say, "Slips don't always lead to slides." He was quite accepting of slips. He believed when a person experienced a slip, one could learn from it, and obtain a greater understanding about what triggered the slip. He taught that it was best to acknowledge that the slip had happened and embrace it as an experience to learn from, as it would further one's recovery. He believed slips were a natural part of the recovery process and an important aspect of relapse prevention.

As you work on your recovery you will experience many slips. Some will lead to slides, others will not. These slips can be obstacles if you let them, or you can try to accept them for what they are. Try to utilize them to learn more about your eating issues and the skills you may need to develop to solidify your recovery. If you can see slips as useful and purposeful, you will be able to acknowledge that they have worth. This will help you fear them less and be more open about exploring their meaning.

Slips can provide us with information about the feelings we are having difficulty tolerating. Or they can tell us about our level of skill to cope with life's varied situations. Slips can be a sign that we need to explore a feeling, process an experience, or expand our repertoire of coping skills. Slips can have great value if you explore them. Try to embrace your slips as a normative process in recovery, instead of filling yourself with shame, self-blame, and guilt. Doing so will help you more easily accept the information they can yield about your recovery.

Learning from your slips can also help you to gain knowledge of techniques to employ as you work on relapse prevention. Knowing what trips you up and when will assist you in planning a different route, anticipating or avoiding the bump, or arranging for a co-pilot, if necessary. Talk about and learn from your slips.

Helpful Hint:

Recall your last slip. Talk about it with a therapist or a friend. Review your awareness of your actions or feelings at the time. Was anyone else present? Had you taken care of yourself well prior to the slip? (e.g., Did you have enough rest the night before, eat well, or not abuse any substances? Were you reminded of someone or something significant? Is it an important anniversary of some sort?) This type of questioning can be useful to uncover the helpful information that presents itself in a slip.

Notice the Moon.

One Friday in October, I happened to appreciate the splendor of the harvest moon during a gorgeous mosquito-free autumn evening. Some neighbors across the street were using their wood stove. The smell of the burning wood was an ever-so-pleasant scent that seemed to amplify the intensity of connecting with nature in this quiet moment. I took a seat on my front steps and paused to soak in the whole incredible vision above me. I thought about some of my life's big questions as well as the spiritual meaning of the moon captivating my gaze that night. Time passed and I eventually went inside, not having answered all of my questions, but definitely reassured about the significance of the bigger picture in life and a little less consumed about the details that concerned me on that given evening.

The next morning I arrived at my office to conduct a women's eating disorder group for the Massachusetts Eating Disorder Association whose group membership varied in age, severity, and type of eating disorder. At the group's onset, one member whose eating disorder was all too consuming of her thoughts, actions, and feelings shouted out with much excitement, "Hey did anyone get a glimpse of the moon last night?" This woman spoke at length about how captivating she found it to be and described eloquently how, for some moments in time, as she peered up at the moon, she was distracted from her consuming eating disorder obsessions. At that moment she had an insight about what life after recovery could be like. She imagined it as experiencing life without the intrusions of her eating disorder voice. It was this image which, for some time to come, offered her motivation and desire to battle her eating disorder voice. It was the "glimpse of the moon" that gave her a "glimpse of recovery." This client's appreciation of the moon had answered one of her life's questions and allowed her to have focus and perspective to guide her recovery. Anyone who battles with eating concerns needs to find their focus, their special reason or reasons for working so hard to recover. Look out at the moon—perhaps you will discover your focus for recovery.

Helpful Hint:

Seek out opportunities to focus on the big pictures of life instead of the day-to-day grind. Immerse yourself in nature. It is amazing how easily we can put our life's worries in perspective with nature in the background. Go to the beach, hike a trail in a state park, watch a sunrise or sunset, or see one of the world's natural wonders. Ponder about what gives your life meaning in the presence of natural beauty. What are your long-term goals? What are your someday wishes? How do you wish to be recalled by others?

Perfection and Certainty Do Not Exist.

How many times have you labored over a project, a paper, your hair, make-up, or a speech in search of perfection, only to lose valuable time, energy, and resources? How many hours have you spent contemplating a difficult decision trying to make certain you have made the right choice? How frequently do you engage in self-abusive or destructive behaviors trying to obtain the perfect body? Well here is an important fact I hope will offer you some relief: perfection and certainty do not exist! So stop exhausting yourself trying to realize them.

You may ask yourself how you came to believe that perfection and certainty are possible. The fostering of this belief is a very smart marketing ploy of the advertising, fashion, and beauty industries. It is estimated that these industries invest billions of dollars each year to promote the myth of perfection. When you buy into the myth and use their products, they will then sell . . . sell . . . sell . . . and make huge amounts of money. They are simply advertising a false product, and reaping very large profits from its sale. These industries bombard us with messages about how various products and services can help us to achieve the perfect look, life, body, relationship, attitude, financial status, grades, and much more if we only use their products. They sell it, we buy it, and every industry with something to sell, including the advertising companies, makes money. Perfection and certainty do not exist; buyers beware!

The Only Thing That Is Constant Is Change.

The fall season is a great time of year. The air turns cooler. The leaves turn beautiful shades of orange, yellow, and red. And there is nothing like throwing on a big sweater and going to an outdoor football game or for a long walk in the woods. This is a change welcomed by most each year. But there are many others changes in life we accept less willingly than the change of seasons. These tend to be changes that are less in our control, for instance, the loss of a loved one, a friendship ending, or a nice vacation coming to an end. While these adjustments are difficult, one needs to realize that the only thing constant in life is change.

Many individuals with eating concerns have trouble with change. The feelings associated with transition—anxiety, fear, and uncertainty—are uncomfortable and can make one feel out of control. Excessive dieting, exercising, or bingeing and purging may start as a misdirected attempt to control change in one's life. Therefore, many eating disorders begin during a time of major transition, such as going to a new high school, starting college, or entering the adult workforce. By focusing on food and weight, one may temporarily avoid feeling the mixed emotions associated with these inevitable life passages. The problem is these feelings are normal—they need not be controlled or numbed out, but must be felt. It is important to experience the feelings associated with change and to pass through them for personal growth and development to occur.

Our society also has trouble with change. We are bombarded with messages telling us our bodies should not change over time. The multibillion-dollar beauty and fashion industry is based on the concept that the aging process can be controlled. The idea of naturally progressing from an adolescent girl, to a young woman, to a mature older woman is to be avoided at all costs. Think about all the anti-aging creams, anti-wrinkle lotions, botox treatments, and plastic surgery options available for sale. Without all these products would the beauty and fashion industry be so profitable? But no matter how much money we spend or time we devote to fighting the aging process, it still happens. Our bodies are constantly changing. It is natural, and it is healthy, to look different at ages 15, 25, and 45.

So the next time you are faced with a change, try to embrace it. Know that change is normal. Instead of focusing on the anxiety produced by the change, focus on the excitement of the unknown. What new opportunities will come of this change? Where will the path lead? Life is like a good mystery novel. There are many twists and turns in the plot. But in the end, the mystery is solved, and, for the most part, you have fun along the way.

Helpful Hint:

Write two lists. On one list all the things that have stayed constant in your life over the past five years, and on the other list all the things that have changed over the past five years. Look at each list. Which list is longer? Which list contains things that have helped you to learn and grow as a person? What would your life have been like if these changes had not occurred? Use this list to gain insight into how you are affected by change and how you can learn to embrace it.

Pursue Your Passion.

Recovered individuals from our eating disorder practice often tell us recovery happened for them in the process of pursuing their passion. Passion is what gives your life meaning. It can fill our emptiness, give us joy, or recharge us when times are daunting. Many recovered individuals talk about needing to find a passion to replace the comfort and fulfillment their disordered eating behaviors once provided in their lives. They talk of the necessity of finding a healthy new passion or reconnecting with an old one that rejuvenates and satisfies them.

Passion comes in all sorts of colors, shapes, and sizes. Some find it in politics, religion, a hobby, or a sport. Others find it in their profession, volunteer work, or an educational pursuit. No matter what your choice of passion is, it is a key to living a balanced, gratifying, and fulfilling life. It is important, however, that you assess this passion for its healthiness for you. Sometimes those who suffer from food and weight issues confuse passion with obsessive compulsions. A useful tip to make this assessment is to ask yourself, "Do you feel that your selected passion is in control of you or are you in control of it?"

Finding your passion can take some effort. Often it emerges as a part of self-discovery. It is helpful to begin by getting it touch with what excites you, what interests you, or what moves you. Pursuing these paths, no matter how slight a feeling they may start off with, can lead to discovering your passion. For example, someone might be aware that they enjoy flowers. They discover that when they have bought some that their spirits picked up. They noticed the presence of flowers cheered them. So they started a small flower garden. Then they took a perennial gardening class at a local nursery, which lead to their joining their local garden club, and they connected with a life passion of gardening. This path seemed to start from an awareness of liking flowers. Begin to pursue your passion. You can start with just an awareness of a simple pleasure.

Helpful Hint:

Periodically thumb through magazines, newspapers, and catalogues and tear out or circle anything that peaks your interest or excites you. Do not edit or use restraint. Anything goes! Notice if there is a pattern or common thread to what you have collected. For example, did you tear out many pictures of animals? Perhaps try volunteering at an animal shelter. Did you notice that you were drawn to some ads for dance classes? Maybe signing up for a tap dancing class could be the place to start. Did you remember you have always wanted to learn how to sail, and now the next town over is offering a free sailing lesson as part of their community boating program?

Desserts Equals Stressed Spelled Backwards.

Learning healthy ways of managing your stress is vital to recovery. Many of us have learned to eat in response to problems and have not had a chance to try non-food-related techniques of relaxation. Dad yells at you, you eat a piece of pie. You get in a fight with your partner, and you inhale the new flavor of Ben and Jerry's ice cream. A bad day at work turns into a night of bingeing and purging.

Where do you think the idea of eating our stress away comes from? Why do we connect dessert (aka "bad" food) with stress management? Just watch television for an evening and you will quickly discover how many commercials give us this message. One advertisement for a major supermarket showed a gigantic ice cream cone with over fifteen scoops of ice cream. As each scoop of ice cream was added to the cone, a comment such as "this is for the fight with the boyfriend" or "this is for the boss who won't give you a raise" is made. The "not so hidden" message is that ice cream can help you with your problems. Although ice cream can be pleasurable, chances are you will eat more ice cream than you normally would, then feel sick to your stomach, and still be in a disagreement with your boyfriend or feel financial stress because of a cheap boss.

Television and the mass media are not the only ones to blame. Many of us grew up in families where dessert or sweets were used as a reward. Little Johnny skinned his knee. A big glass of milk and chocolate chip cookies will "make it all better." Jenny got an "A" on her spelling test, so a piece of grandma's apple pie is in order. What we learn over time is desserts are to be eaten to take the pain away or to celebrate a victory. At the same time we are taught dessert foods are "bad" and are to be avoided, at all costs. But it is okay to crave a cookie and have one. It is okay to eat for pleasure.

Chances are bakery items will always be used by moms and dads to nurture, to ease a child's pain, or celebrate a birthday. The definition of normal eating includes eating food for pleasure and comfort. It can be one of life's simple pleasures. But it is important that children, and adults, learn other ways of managing stressful situations besides gorging themselves on dessert or denying themselves a treat. Sometimes a walk in the park can be a better way to unwind from a stressful workday than sitting in front of the television eating bon-bons. Take your child to the beach for a game of Frisbee to celebrate a good report card. Quietly read a good book to distract yourself from an argument with a friend.

The next time you crave a sugary binge food, remember desserts equals stressed spelled backwards. Try to determine if you are craving a cookie for emotional reasons or physical reasons. If the craving started after a fight with dad, you may want to use another coping strategy. If you desire a big piece of pie because it smells good and would hit the spot, dig right in!

Helpful Hint:

Learn the simple stress management technique of deep breathing. Research shows taking a few deep breaths can help reduce your stress level almost immediately. If you need help learning it, sign up for a class on stress management at your local community center, take a yoga class at the local YMCA, or buy a relaxation tape or book.

Walk to the Beat of Your Own Drum.

You may have heard of this famous quote, "Walk to the beat of a different drummer." I always mistakenly quoted it as "Walk to the beat of your own drum," perhaps due to my phonetic learning disability. When I finally learned the actual quotation, I thought the anonymous writer would appreciate my twist. We are all unique individuals of various weights, shapes, and heights. We have personality differences as well as socioeconomic, political, ethnic, religious, and sexual differences. As no two snowflakes are alike, neither are any two people. Be proud of your differences, personal twists, and imperfections. Listen to your heart, and trust your gut. Live life walking at your own pace, listen to your own groove, and be proud about it. Walk to the beat of your own drum!

Helpful Hint:

Consider that many of the world's greatest contributors were people who walked down paths where no one else ventured, despite what their contemporaries thought. Discover your unique contributions when you walk to the beat of your own drum. Dare to be different.

Every Day Is a Gift.

It would be wonderful if we could view every day as a gift to be cherished. Instead many of us wake up with thoughts such as, "I have so much to do and so little time"; "I hope I don't blow my diet today"; or "How am I going to make it through another day with food?" These automatic thoughts do not make us want to jump for joy at the prospect of a new day. Instead these negative words lead us to feel depressed, anxious, and unsatisfied with our lives. Often we forget what a miracle each day is. That each morning we awake with the ability to breathe, walk, talk, and spend time enjoying life.

As a teenager I did not understand my father's optimism. He practiced daily the philosophy that life is a gift. I remember waking up sleepy-eyed and walking into the bathroom to get ready for school. At the time I considered a day in high school like a day on the frontlines of a battlefield—not a lot of fun. I would stumble through the upstairs hallway, and my father would greet me with a big smile and shout, "Good morning! Isn't today a great day to be alive!" I would growl at him to leave me alone and be off with my negative thoughts. As a warrior prepares for battle, I was preparing for another day in combat (aka high school). As an adult, I would greet the day in the same way I did as a teen, with dread and anxiety over what I had to do, what I could not do, what I wish I had time to do. My day would start with a negative attitude, which often led to negative feelings and would result in a mediocre day at best. At night I would crawl into bed exhausted by my own thoughts and pull the covers over my head in relief.

On a few occasions, despite my negative approach to life, something would happen that would shift my thoughts from depreciating to appreciating the world. One day I was rushing to a job I did not like. I was thinking about how unfair life was and how I was going to have a bad day. All of sudden a family of ducks walked in front of my car. I slammed on my brakes and luckily avoided hitting the ducklings. When forced to slow down, I noticed the humor and the joy in watching these ducks waddle across the road from one pond to another. I laughed out loud at how comical it was to see angry commuters stopped by this duck family. Along with the other commuters, I had to wait for the ducks to slowly pass by. They were not in a rush because I had a job to go to. They were in the moment focused on making it from one side of the road to the other. One by one they were enjoying the journey to the new pond.

As I began moving forward again, I noticed the sun rising on the water and the beautiful way the light hit the shore. I noticed the ducks and how rare it was to be able to see a snapshot of nature in the hustle and bustle of the morning commute. I remember smiling and feeling the tension lift from my shoulders as my body relaxed. It was as if I was given a gift from Mother Nature to help me slow down, become more balanced, and enjoy the day.

Since that experience, I have tried to stop and smell the roses. I try to replace the negative thoughts with positive ones. For I have found, as many of my clients have discovered, your thoughts can change your feelings and your experience. What was once a dreaded commute to a dead-end job, turned into a pleasurable drive to work at a job I would hold until I could find more satisfying work. The way in which I thought about it, helped empower me to pursue my dreams.

At times I still forget to view life as optimistically as my father does. But I do try to remember his words and repeat them to myself when I least want to. I also focus on the small stuff: the sunlight, the squirrels playing in the backyard, the relaxing sound of rain falling on the roof. All of these things help remind me I am lucky to be alive, that life truly is a gift, and that each day I should slowly unwrap the day to discover the surprise within.

Helpful Hint:

Keep a "gift" journal. At the end of each day write down three gifts you received during the day. Examples might include a smile from a stranger, someone holding the door open for you, or a chance to notice the sunset. No matter how small life's gifts are, keeping a log will help you remember them and help refocus you in a positive direction.

Life after Recovery Is Just Life.

Many women have an idealized view of recovery. When asked to describe what a day would be like fully recovered, a person often describes a day filled with relaxation and joy. Maybe because many women with eating concerns are perfectionists, they see recovery as a state of perfection. In reality, life after recovery is just life.

Life for all people involves up and downs. Some days are trying. The dishes need to be washed. The kids are crying. The term paper is overdue. Your partner is annoying you. Your job is stressful. There is no milk for your coffee. This is life. Some days are filled with precious moments to be savored. A special day spent with a loved one. The feeling one gets on her wedding day. The calmness of a day spent just hanging out with a trusted friend. A cozy day lying on the couch watching snowflakes float from the sky onto the backyard lawn.

Recovery does not exempt you from the problems of daily living, nor does it guarantee a life filled only with joy. It is normal to experience sorrow as well as elation. The process of getting well has taught you what you need to know to cope with the highs and the lows. You have learned what feelings and thoughts need to be paid attention to, the ways to cope with the feelings and how to nurture yourself along the way. While life after recovery is not picture perfect, it can be perfectly wonderful.

Helpful Hint:

Ask three trusted friends to describe what life is like for them on a daily basis. Choose friends who are either fully recovered or those whom you consider realistic role models or mentors. Ask them the following questions:

1. What parts of life do you enjoy?
2. What parts of life do you find challenging?
3. How do you cope with each?

Chances are their answers will reveal not perfection, but a realistic view of what life may be like after recovery.

Recovery Is Possible.

Some professionals think eating disorders are like alcoholism or drug addiction, in that you are an addict and will always be an addict. In our experience, this is not true. While using food to cope with life's problems can become an addictive behavior, the substance, food, is not addictive. You can learn to normalize your eating and break the cycle of bingeing, purging, and/or restricting. Over the many years we have been treating men and women with eating concerns and working in the field of eating disorders, we have witnessed hundreds of people fully recover.

As we previously mentioned, the road to recovery can be long, winding, and uncertain. When you lose faith, it may feel like you will never live a life free of food and weight obsession. But stay hopeful. We often tell our clients we will hold onto the hope of recovery for them until they are ready to hold hope for themselves. When you feel discouraged, reach out to the many sources of inspiration. Local and national eating disorders nonprofit groups, such as the National Eating Disorders Association (NEDA), sponsor recovery panels, workshops, and support groups. Locate one in your area and go. While everyone's journey is different, there is no substitute for meeting someone who has been there and has made it past her eating problem. If you cannot find a recovery panel or a support group in your area, there are many books that talk about recovery and how it is not only possible, but probable. Lastly, the Internet provides some websites to help you connect with treatment and get support. Most sites contain information, resources, and chat rooms for the person with the eating concern, as well as for parents, spouses, and loved ones. Beware of websites that cater to your unhealthy side. We have included a list of our favorite websites in the resource section of this book. Each are sponsored by great organizations dedicated to helping prevent and treat eating concerns and each has been used by our clients.

We hope you have found this book helpful in your journey. Remember, being discouraged is part of the process. But also remember this book was written because we know you can conquer your eating concerns. No matter what type of eating problem you are facing, we are confident that with professional treatment, time, support, and determination, you can fully recover. RECOVERY IS POSSIBLE!

The Loved
One's Journey

Be a Super Model.

It is important to be a good role model for your children. Those who struggle with anorexia, bulimia, and binge-eating disorders are often hypervigilant to the actions of parents and significant others in their life. They may watch others to affirm and solidify the new self-messages and healthy behaviors they are working on in therapy. Be aware of your actions and your language. You can be a conduit for change in your daughter's life if you are consistent with the messages of recovery. Being a super model means no dieting, no cursing your body, or judging others by their appearances. It is adopting a healthy exercise regime, eating for nutrition's sake as well as, at times, for pleasure. It is a lifestyle of maintaining a balance between work and play, graciously accepting your limits and your own imperfections.

We are a significant influence on our children. Consider your actions and how they may impact or give mixed messages to your child who is struggling to combat her eating disorder voice. Are you encouraging your child to eat, yet for dinner you sit down to a diet, frozen dinner entrée? Are you lamenting how you look in that blue dress you bought last summer, yet trying to convince your daughter she doesn't look fat in her swimsuit? Do you resolve that fight with your boss by ordering and eating a whole Boston cream pie for lunch, while you try to coax her to listen to her body and eat only when she is hungry, not for emotional comfort?

In short, it is important to be aware of how your actions affirm the messages of your daughter's recovery, and how your words emulate what your behavior is exemplifying. Strive to be a good role model of healthy behaviors.

Helpful Hint:

Look at yourself in the mirror. What do your behaviors, language, and judgments of others reflect to your eating disordered child? Notice what you are doing well, also observe what areas you may need improvement. Consider getting a consultation from a therapist who works with parents of eating disordered individuals. Our resource section at the end of this book can assist you on how to find one.

Educate for Your Children's Sake.

Many psychosocial problems young people face today are being addressed by early intervention efforts. Think of the ads we see on television about talking to your children about drugs and alcohol before they hit those years when peer pressure is so influential. Or consider how colleges and high schools are now including date rape prevention lectures in their health classes and orientation programs. Many organizations have developed prevention strategies and early intervention tactics as a means to combat a significant number of growing social concerns. They have concluded what studies have confirmed: Talking with and educating your children early, about the dangers of various behaviors, can help to prevent them.

Many eating disorders therapists and educators have developed excellent early intervention school curriculum. Their curriculum espouses the importance of talking with your children and those who are in their circle of influence, including friends, teachers, coaches, and neighbors regarding the genetics of body diversity, the dangers of dieting, and the medical consequences one can suffer from eating disorder behaviors. It is important to dispel myths that the general population floats out there such as "fat people are fat because they eat too much," or "a thin person is healthier than a fat one." We should look to affirm that imperfection is normal and should be accepted as human occurrence, not cursed. Your child does not live in isolation and is exposed to many outside influences. Talking with as many of the people they interact with when the opportunity presents itself will have an impact. At the very least, you will have greater insight as to who in your child's life is a healthy role model.

In addition, we need to teach our children to be media literate. Media literacy is a term applied to the concept of teaching people to be educated consumers. It helps them to see the hidden messages in advertisements that serve to manipulate and direct the viewer to buy goods and services. We need to talk to our children about these tactics and help them to see that the images of beauty, wealth, success, and happiness portrayed are unrealistic and over-idealized. These images are depicted as such solely to sell. We can achieve this aim by talking with our children, much as we teach them why the toy they saw on television is not quite that large in real life, or will not work as well when they get it home, or is just not as much fun as it seemed to be in the advertisement.

Helpful Hint:

Talk to your children and educate them about the dangers of dieting, eating disorder behaviors, and about how the messages portrayed in the media may affect them. Consider spearheading efforts to get an educational program included in your child's school curriculum. There are several good resources available including *Healthy Body Image: Teaching Kids to Eat and Love Their Bodies Too!*, by Kathy Kater (EDAP, 1998); and *Go Girls Eating Disorders Awareness and Prevention*, by the National Eating Disorders Association (EDAP, 1999).

Watch for Red Flags.

Statistics from the National Eating Disorders Association report almost half of American elementary school students between first and third grades want to be thinner. Four out of five children at the age of ten are afraid of being fat. Half of nine- and ten-year-old girls feel better about themselves if they are on a diet. At any given time, one half of American women report being on a diet, and one in four men report the same. It is additionally reported that 35 percent of all "normal dieters" will progress to pathological dieting, and one in four will progress to a partial or fully developed eating disorder.

We need to watch for red flags that our daughters, sons, sisters, brothers, or significant others may be getting into trouble with their dieting. Know the common symptoms of anorexia, bulimia, and binge-eating disorders. Listen to your child's language about her body, her concerns about her physical development, and her reaction to weight shifts. Hear the meaning behind her comments about her body, her attitudes about weight loss or gains, and the body images she idealizes. Pay attention to behaviors that may be signs of your daughter's obsession with dieting or pursuit of thinness. Has your child's interest in nutritional labels recently peaked? Is she suddenly declaring herself to be a vegetarian? Do you find an abundance of food wrappers in her knapsack? Is she staying up late at night to exercise when she thinks you are asleep? Don't be afraid to ask your children about what you are observing and what it means to them. We have found early intervention is a principal factor in recovery from eating disorders. It is important to trust your instincts when some red flags are posted and for you to address the potential danger.

Helpful Hint:

Monitor and talk to your child if you are noticing red flags. Watch for opportunities to teach her healthy messages. Seek a professional evaluation if your gut feeling tells you to. Keep in mind that it may be better to have an evaluation that indicates no reason to be concerned, rather than waiting too long and having an eating disorder become well entrenched.

Crisis Brings Opportunity.

According to the American Heritage Dictionary, the definition of crisis is, "a crucial point or situation in the course of anything; *a turning point.*" This is an important definition for parents and partners to remember as their loved one travels the bumpy road of recovery. While no one wishes for a crisis, it can be a time of tremendous growth and learning for the person with eating concerns.

Think of times in your life when a crisis has occurred. Did you lose a loved one? Get fired or laid off from your job? Drop out of college or school? While this time in your life probably was emotionally difficult, it was a turning point. The predicament can result in two things happening that may be beneficial. First, you may become more open to change. If you are secure in your job, but not in love with it, it may be hard to take the risk of looking for a more rewarding position. But if you lose the same mediocre job, by necessity, you are open to change and possibly you will be more willing to be creative in the directions you are willing to turn. Second, a crisis time yields insights that would otherwise not be revealed. For example, you may not consider why you do not stand up for yourself in relationships unless an unhealthy relationship ends. Sometimes the pain of the crisis gets us to ask ourselves those tough questions.

How does this apply to eating disorders treatment and recovery? Think about when you first noticed your loved one was having a problem with food. Chances are some sort of crisis brought it to your attention. It may have been in the form of a telephone call from a school guidance counselor concerned about your child's decreasing grades, social isolation, and/or weight loss. It may be a partner getting fired and then telling you for the first time they were leaving work several hours early each day to compulsively exercise. It could be a visit to the emergency room after a loved one faints and you are told they have been bingeing and purging and need help. While the event is painful for all involved, it can lead the person with anorexia, bulimia, or compulsive overeating to ask for help for the first time. It is truly a turning point.

Often it takes a family, personal, or treatment crisis to lead to lasting change and growth. Just like with other types of crises, it is an opportunity for change to happen. It may allow your loved one to be more open to recognizing the damage the eating disorder has done to their health, as well as the health of the family. It is a time when a person contemplating recovery may finally begin to let go of symptoms and try new healthier ways of coping with the world. So the next time a crisis comes along, remember crisis brings opportunity.

Helpful Hint:

Write the saying "Crisis brings opportunity" on a piece of paper. Post it somewhere you are going to see each day. Read it often.

Get Out of the Blame Game.

When a child or a loved one is diagnosed with an eating disorder, it is natural for parents, spouses, and friends to ask why, and to look for someone or something to blame. Many parents spend countless hours worrying they caused their loved one's eating problems. They believe that if they find out what they did wrong, they can correct it and make the eating disorder go away.

Eating disorders, like life, are not simple. Family life may be a contributor, but it is never the sole cause. The development of an eating disorder is complex. Imagine you are building a house of cards. As each card is placed in position, it either adds to the strength of the house or weakens it. Eventually all the cards will be resting on each other, balancing precariously on the table. You go to place the last card and the house crashes to the ground. Was the final card to blame for the collapse? No. It was all the cards and how they were stacked together to make the house that lead to its demise.

Now picture your family as the house of cards. The eating disorder hits your loved one like the final card being placed on the house of cards. Once again, no one person in the family caused the eating problem. It was a combination of factors including what has, and is happening in the family, the person's genetic predisposition toward eating disordered behaviors, the individual's personality style and life experiences. Still, many parents feel responsible for a child's problem with food, and fear they are to blame. A lot of time is spent worrying about what they could have done better or differently to spare their loved one and their family the pain an eating disorder inflicts. Some parents are resistant to family therapy, believing the sessions will be one big blame game. But there is no single cause; no one person to blame. Family therapy helps the entire family look at this and learn how to work together toward recovery.

It takes time and energy to play the blame game. A better use of your personal resources would be to educate yourself about the complexity of eating disorders. Be brave. Engage in therapy when asked. Be a support system for your loved one and get support for yourself. It feels much better to stop the blame and get into the recovery game.

Helpful Hint:

Take an old deck of cards and cover the face of the cards with construction paper. On each card use a marker to indicate a person, place, or thing, which is part of your family system. On a card, put your name, your loved ones', your spouse's, the dog's, the move to a new town, low self-esteem, breakup with a boyfriend, the first diet, genetics, perfectionism, and so on. In the end you will have a deck of your family's house of cards. Now start building your card house. Notice how each card touches another card; each influences the other. Keep building the house until it finally crashes. Observe how the final card was not to blame, but only a contributor to the demise of the whole network of cards. Each time you find yourself playing the blame game, get out the deck of cards and start building!

Pace Yourself.

Recovery from an eating disorder can take many years; therefore, it is important to pace yourself accordingly. It is very difficult to watch someone you love suffer, to see their isolation, their missed opportunities, and the damage they have done to their bodies. To be a steadfast supporter involves learning how to pace yourself and give yourself permission to ask for help from a professional, a supportive friend, or another worried family member.

In light of our experience treating those with eating disorders, you can be a significant player on your loved one's treatment team. Your presence can offer connection when they feel most isolated, encouragement when they want to give up, and hope when they have run out of it. However, it is impossible for any one person to provide all of this. That is one reason why your loved one is best treated in a team approach. Each member of the team has a role to play, which serves an important function, not only to the one who suffers from the eating disorder, but to each other as well.

It is important not to give up; so try to pace yourself. Watch your energy level. Recognize the battle your loved one is fighting is tough and emotionally draining at times. The reality of any long-term problem is it takes a toll on everyone. It is all right to ask for help. It is okay to be honest about your feelings, your worries, and your needs. If you are finding it difficult to be a mainstay supporter, talk with your loved one and tell them you need to take a step back or take a momentary break. Recognize that you, like everyone else, have limitations. If you need space, take it. If you need education regarding understanding the symptoms, get it. If you need someone to cry to, find a shoulder. Recovery is a process which can include many people. You don't always have to be the cheerleader, inspirer, or confronter. Support yourself and your loved one by developing a good treatment team.

Helpful Hint:

Envision yourself training for a marathon. Recognize the
importance of determining the pace you must set to
complete the marathon. Some runners seek professional
coaches to help them set a healthy pace, particularly for
when they encounter rougher terrain or are approaching the
finish line. Use this image to help you, as you walk with
your loved one, in their recovery marathon.

Have Hope.

Hope is crucial for our loved ones who are struggling to overcome their eating and body concerns. Working toward recovery can take years, particularly if one has gone untreated for a long time. For those who battle to recover, hope can easily be lost. In moments of despair, it is vital for them to have someone close to them carry the hope. Your loved one will need to know that someone in their life has confidence that they will figure things out, and eventually live symptom free. It is not important to have the answers; it is important to believe in their ability to uncover the answers for themselves. They will utilize the strength of your hope, until they have enough belief in themselves.

Without hope of recovery, it can be difficult to take that next step or to try again to achieve what one feels she has already tried before, without success. It is important to have someone on your loved one's team who has hope and confidence that recovery is possible. If this is not present on your loved one's treatment team, assist your loved one in finding treatment providers that do believe recovery is possible. Although you cannot control or direct the actual work of recovery, you can provide an environment that encourages your loved one to continue her efforts. This encouragement is often a good source of energy to fuel the battle. By having hope, even when there seems to be none, you can provide the vigor and inspiration for your loved one to try a technique yet again, combat that eating disorder voice, or agree to get that recommended treatment. People do get better. Recovery is possible. Have hope.

Helpful Hint:

Locate a local or national eating disorders association. These organizations are often a great resource for materials and events that offer messages of hope and inspiration. There are many state and national organizations that have been founded for the purpose of treatment and prevention of eating disorders. Frequently organizations will sponsor a forum in which a panel of recovered individuals will share their personal stories of recovery. National Eating Disorders Awareness Week, celebrated in February each year, also features many events at local hospitals, schools, and college campuses which offer programs to encourage. Attend one of these forums.

The Professional's Journey

Recovery Is a Team Sport.

Can you imagine winning a football game without a team? It would be you on the scrimmage line against eleven players. What are the odds of you gaining yardage, let alone winning the game? Pretty small, if at all.

The same odds are true in the recovery. As clinicians, we need to work as a member of an eating disorders treatment team. Just like in football, each team is composed of different players with different specialties. The quarterback may be the individual therapist, while the center is the physician; and the other positions may consist of the nutritionist, the family therapist, the group therapist, and if applicable, the guidance counselor, school staff, and sports coach. The linemen, who block and allow the play to be completed, could consist of the family and friends who support the client in recovery. Lastly, the receiver, the most important part of the team, is the client. With the support of the team, the client can reach the long-term goal—full recovery.

Why is a team important in work with clients with eating concerns? The nature of the illness is multifaceted. Each client faces individual and family psychological issues, medical concerns, and nutritional deficits. The team works to address all of these areas simultaneously. No one person can play all these roles effectively.

When the team works together, it will develop a rhythm over time, which will be helpful to the client and to each team member. Hopefully, as any sports teams do, the treatment team will learn from its mistakes and practice what works again and again. Effective communication and good sportsmanship are vital. All members should be involved in developing an effective treatment strategy; each contributing to his or her area of expertise.

Just as in sports, the game is never won on a single play. It takes time and various interventions to help a client achieve full recovery. Sometimes, all of the team members will be involved; at others, only a few. For example, a client diagnosed with anorexia is at a low weight and medical stability is one of the primary treatment concerns. The goal of weight restoration for physical and emotional health is paramount. This client will be monitored weekly by the physician and seen weekly by the nutritionist and therapist. The physician performs weekly lab work and vital readings to ensure that the client can be treated safely on an outpatient basis. He or she works closely with the nutritionist, who helps the client to slowly increase food intake in order to maintain and increase medical stability and so that the client can cognitively do the therapeutic work. The individual therapist meets with the client to process the feelings she has in this intensive outpatient model, as well as to continue to uncover what the underlying psychological issues are that led the person to self-starvation.

As the client progresses in recovery, the team may change its emphasis. The nutritionist and the physician may be less involved as the client's medical health improves. A family therapist or group therapist may become more involved in the treatment as the shift toward the psychological issues intensifies. Collaborate with your client and the team to determine which team members and which specialty areas to focus on at any given time.

At times teams may have trouble working together. This may cause the treatment to become fragmented. Families can become confused and frustrated and clients may be allowed to continue unhealthy behaviors or dynamics. If this is the case, have a team meeting and try to strategize to resolve problems as quickly as possible. Make your treatment team a win-win situation for you, your colleagues, and your client.

Helpful Hint:

Get involved with a local or national eating disorders nonprofit group or an eating disorders peer supervision group. It is a great way to meet other team players, get professional support, and learn more about resources in your area. If you do not know where to start, look at the resource section in this book for some of our favorite organizations.

Sometimes Appearances Do Count.

In the years of working with clients with eating concerns, we hear ourselves saying over and over again, "It's what's on the inside that counts." While we believe this with all our hearts, we are also aware that a picture conveys a thousand words. As clinicians, we need to realize first impressions and appearances do count. These images can help our clients trust us or get in the way of the therapy we are doing.

I learned this lesson the hard way in the first year of graduate school. I was interning at a college counseling center and working with a young woman named Isabella on body image issues and eating concerns. She had been coming in for sessions for about 8 weeks, when one day she questioned me regarding what I told her with my words, versus what she saw me do with my behaviors. Isabella and I were talking about how important it was in recovery to get away from diet foods and focus on what your physical cues tell you to eat. She looked at me with a confused expression and stated, "If that is true, why do you drink Diet Sprite?" She pointed to the can of diet soda on my desk. I do not remember my response, but I do know that it was not a brilliant therapeutic intervention.

Isabella taught me an important lesson: Look at the unspoken messages and images in my office and see what I am conveying to my clients in a nonverbal way. As clinicians we are not only counseling clients with our words, we are helping them—or unintentionally hurting them—through our actions.

Helpful Hint:

Imagine you are a new client entering your office for the first time. Sit in the waiting room. Are the chairs comfortable for all body sizes? Read the magazines. Are the images and articles consistent with what is discussed in your therapy sessions? Look at the pictures on the walls. What do you see? Are the nonverbal messages supportive of recovery? If so, keep doing it. If not, think about how to make your office a more supportive recovery zone. If the changes are cost-prohibitive or outside of your control (e.g., sharing your office with other clinicians), talk with your clients about it. Teach them how to cope in a world, which so often bombards them with messages that conflict with therapeutic goals.

Plant the Seed; You Never Know What Will Grow.

The ambivalence inherent in clients with eating concerns sometimes makes us question our therapeutic effectiveness. Individuals enter treatment with varying levels of readiness for the work. It is our job to assess their readiness for change and make our interventions accordingly. Some clients will move from denial to termination in our office. Others may come to us when they are contemplating giving up their eating disorders and leave before taking action to do so. We need to remember that part of the process of eating disorders treatment is to plant seeds of wisdom in our sessions and to know that some day, they will blossom. At times, some clients blossom before our eyes. Others clients do so in our colleagues' offices.

Part of the role of a clinician is to be a nurturer. To educate our clients, express concern for their medical and emotional well-being, and to gently nudge them when they need to be pushed to take the next step. At times, we wonder if our clients hear what we are saying. A good example is a client that has been in therapy with me for many years. She struggles with depression and compulsive overeating. For years, I would mention cognitive behavioral techniques to address the irrational beliefs that fueled both her mood and eating disorder. Each time these techniques were mentioned to counteract mind reading, personalization, or "should" statements (all types of irrational beliefs), she would roll her eyes and say, "That cognitive stuff does not work for me." Time passed by, and in the context of our nurturing relationship, she grew personally. Her depression, while still present, lessened and her eating became more normalized. One day, after she had become more comfortable in therapy, she was describing an incident that had happened over the weekend when she stopped and said to me, "I don't like to admit it, but I guess this cognitive behavioral stuff actually works." The seed had been planted and with time, nurturance, and patience it had grown.

Helpful Hint:

To work in the field of eating disorders, it is important to examine your therapeutic expectations of yourself and your client. Being realistic and mindful that part of your work is to plant seeds that in time will grow can take the burden to fix the problem off you as a therapist and allow you to be a helpful part of the process. Supervision groups are great for helping you determine what is feasible and what may be wishful thinking. Join an existing one or start one with a few colleagues. It can be fun to garden together!

Take Tea and See.

As a little girl, I had a very beloved Great Aunt Josie who was a robust Sicilian Catholic woman. She offered loving wisdom as frequently as she felt her pearls were needed. She could spot a worried look, a disconcerted youngster, or an accident ready to happen from far across any room. She was always interested in attending to any one of these concerns, no matter how young or old the person was, whether they were a dear family member, or a new acquaintance. Most memorable of all her pearls of wisdom was a frequently quoted phrase I fully understood only long after her death—"Take tea and see."

Indeed my coming to understand this notion over time exactly illustrated her meaning of the phrase. What I came to learn was that sometimes when you are anxious about whether something will work, or you are laboring over a difficult decision, or you are just working hard to develop insight and understanding, it is helpful to take a break. Eventually the worry may dissipate, the answer may reveal itself, or knowledge may emerge. With time we will become enlightened. The act of taking a break, slowing down, allowing maturation, or simply coming up for air is often the process through which we come to know things. Sometimes this is a process we are quite aware of and it is very deliberate, like enjoying a chat with a good friend over a cup of tea to take your mind off your troubles, and later discovering that you have a new outlook. At other times, it is less conscious, like the gradual acquisition of understanding, which can emerge as we grow, learn, and mature.

Many people who seek treatment are often consumed with worry and anxiety about starting treatment. They often present numerous questions such as, "Why do I possess an eating disorder or use eating disorder behaviors?" They pressure the therapist for quick, specific answers. These people need to learn that discovery of their unique answers will unfold over time, and that such answers are not always immediately available to us. It is also useful to help them recognize that, although talking about one's concerns is an important and useful practice in treatment, it can be equally useful to take a break from one's symptoms and appreciate the value of other aspects of life. These breaks can be restorative to the sometimes quite diminished hope for recovery. Teaching folks how to "Take a tea and see" will be an important early skill to develop in treatment.

Helpful Hint:

Acknowledge, take stock, and experience the restorative value of taking short breaks in a variety of activities in your life. Rest in between halves of a basketball game, chat with a colleague between sessions, or take a break when you just can't seem to put an "easy to assemble" project together. Notice when you return, your increased energy level, your improved focus, or how those pieces just pop into place. Reflect historically over your life and become aware of how frequently time has just naturally provided you with insight. Sometimes enlightenment and revitalization happen very slowly and microscopically, and they don't reveal themselves until you are ready. You can't force the process.

Change Can Happen One Person at a Time.

The pervasiveness of eating disorders in our society, coupled with the long-term nature of treatment and the short-term nature of managed care, may lead us as professionals to feel overwhelmed and discouraged in our work. When disheartened, it is important to remember change can happen one person at a time.

Imagine a pond or lake on a calm summer day at the beginning of a rain shower. The first raindrop to hit the body of water breaks the surface. The droplet then creates a ripple effect. The surface area impacted by the rain droplet, spreads in size and circumference, eventually reaching out across the water. The same is true with our clinical work. When an individual enters treatment, you educate the client regarding the dangers of dieting and obsession with thinness. You help them transform their unhealthy belief system into a more balanced worldview. This individual work "ripples" as the person recovers and, formally or informally shares her personal story. Family, friends, physicians, school staff, and/or coaches witness, and sometimes participate in, the recovery. They are educated in the process and forever changed. What ultimately started as educating one person in your office has resulted in changing a family system as well as a community.

We also can effect change in the way we live our personal lives. By practicing what we preach, we can model healthy behaviors to our friends and families. Simple things like not engaging in diet conversations with friends or colleagues; not using terms such as fat in derogatory ways, not saying, "I feel fat" when really you are feeling unworthy; and by not judging others, especially our clients, for having a body that may not conform with societal ideals. Be accepting of yourself and others. This approach, too, will have a ripple effect.

Helpful Hint:

On a piece of paper draw an image of a raindrop hitting the water and creating a ripple effect. Now think of one case you are currently working on and put in all the names of people that you have changed by treating one person. For example, you are at the center, and the first concentric circle of impact includes your client. The next ripple could include the client's family, physician, nutritionist, group therapist, and school counselor. As it spreads out, the next circle would include people in the audience at a recovery panel discussion your client participated in. The next includes the future partners and children. Look at the image and see how far and wide your message can go!

Resources

Do I Have an Eating Disorder?*

Do you wonder if you might have an eating disorder, or if you could be on your way to developing one? Ask yourself these questions . . .

- Do you constantly calculate the fat grams and calories you've eaten?
- Do you weigh yourself often and find you are obsessed with the number on the scale?
- Do you exercise because you feel like you have to, not because you want to?
- Do you avoid eating meals or snacks when you're around other people?
- Do you ever feel out of control when you're eating?
- Are you afraid of gaining weight?
- Do your eating patterns include extreme dieting, strong preferences for certain foods, withdrawn or ritualized behavior at mealtime, or secretive bingeing?
- Has weight loss, dieting, and/or control of food become one of your major concerns?
- Do you feel ashamed, disgusted, or guilty after eating?
- Do you spend a significant amount of time worrying about the weight, shape, or size of your body?
- Do you use diet pills, herbal supplements, laxatives, or vomiting as a way to control your weight?
- Do you feel like your identity and value as a person is based on how you look or how much you weigh?

Although this is not meant to be a diagnostic evaluation, if you answered "*yes*" to any of these questions, you could be dealing with, or on

---

* Provided by the National Eating Disorders Association. For more information, contact the National Eating Disorders Association, 603 Stewart Street, Suite 803, Seattle, WA 98101. 1-800-931-2237. www.nationaleatingdisorders.org. Copyright 2001 National Eating Disorders Association. This handout may be copied for educational purposes only.

your way to, an eating disorder. It is important that you start to talk about your body image concerns, eating habits, and exercise patterns now, rather than waiting until your situation gets more serious than you can handle. Tell a friend, teacher, parent, coach, youth group leader, doctor, counselor, or nutritionist what you're going through. It is important to have support as you begin the process of changing thoughts and behaviors and to seek professional help.

What Does Treatment Involve?*

The most effective and long-lasting treatment for an eating disorder is some form of psychotherapy or psychological counseling, coupled with careful attention to medical and nutritional needs. Ideally, this treatment should be tailored to the individual and will vary according to both the severity of the disorder and the patient's particular problems, needs, and strengths.

Psychological counseling must address both the eating disordered symptoms *and* the underlying psychological, interpersonal, and cultural forces that contributed to the eating disorder. Some examples are:

- The individual needs to learn how to live peacefully and healthfully with food and with themselves.
- Typically care is provided by a licensed health professional, including but not limited to a psychologist, psychiatrist, social worker, nutritionist, and/or medical doctor.
- Care should be coordinated and provided by a health professional with expertise and experience in dealing with eating disorders.

Many people with eating disorders respond to outpatient therapy, including individual, group, or family therapy *and* medical management by their primary care provider. Support groups, nutritional counseling, and psychiatric medications under careful medical supervision have also proven helpful for some individuals.

Hospital-based care (including inpatient, partial hospitalization, intensive outpatient and/or residential care in an eating disorders specialty unit or facility) is necessary when an eating disorder has led to

---

*Provided by the National Eating Disorders Association. For more information, contact the National Eating Disorders Association, 603 Stewart Street, Suite 803, Seattle, WA 98101. 1-800-931-2237. www.nationaleatingdisorders.org. Copyright 2001 National Eating Disorders Association. This handout may be copied for educational purposes only.

physical problems that may be life-threatening, or when it is associated with severe psychological or behavioral problems.

The exact treatment needs of each individual will vary. It is important for individuals struggling with an eating disorder to find a health professional they trust to help coordinate and oversee their individual care.

Helpful Questions When Considering Treatment. *

There are many differing approaches to the treatment of eating disorders. No one approach is considered superior for everyone; however, it is important to find an option that is most effective for your needs. The following is a list of questions you might want to ask when contacting eating disorder support services. These questions apply to an individual therapist, treatment facility, other eating disorders support service, or any combination of treatment options.

- How long have you been treating eating disorders?
- Are you licensed? What are your training credentials?
- What is your treatment style?
- What kind of evaluation process will be used in recommending a treatment plan?
- What kind of medical information do you need? Will I need a medical evaluation before entering the program?
- What is your appointment availability? Do you offer after-work or early morning appointments? How long do the appointments last? How often will we meet?
- How long will the treatment process take? When will we know it's time to stop treatment?
- Are you reimbursable by my insurance? What if I don't have insurance or mental health benefits under my health care plan?
- Ask the facility to send information brochures, treatment plans, treatment prices, and so on. The more information the facility is able to send in writing, the better informed you will be.

---

* Provided by the National Eating Disorders Association. For more information, contact the National Eating Disorders Association, 603 Stewart Street, Suite 803, Seattle, WA 98101. 1-800-931-2237. www.nationaleatingdisorders.org. Copyright 2001 National Eating Disorders Association. This handout may be copied for educational purposes only.

With a careful search, the provider you select will be helpful. But, if the first time you meet with him or her is awkward, don't be discouraged. The first few appointments with any treatment provider are often challenging. It takes time to build up trust in someone with whom you are sharing highly personal information. If you continue to feel that you need a different therapeutic environment, you may need to consider other providers.

How to Help a Loved One with an Eating Disorder.

- **Express your concern.** If you are concerned about someone you love having an eating disorder, tell her. Silence will only lead the person to believe that the problem is in her head, or worse yet, does not exist. Express your concerns, focusing on how you feel when you see the person displaying symptoms. Be prepared to listen and remember that denial can be a component of an eating disorder. Do offer to assist in getting your loved one professional help for the problem. Remember the earlier the intervention, the better the prognosis.
- **Get educated.** Read books like this one on eating concerns and learn more about eating disorders and the underlying issues that trigger the behavior. It is important to become knowledgeable about the problem so you can help your loved one recover.
- **Remember food is not the issue.** Focus on you loved one's feelings. If she is restricting, bingeing, or purging she may feel worthless. Fighting about her symptoms will only create a control battle that is not useful. Learn to ask about the emotions behind the symptoms. Remember that if your loved one's food and weight obsession was just about food, you would not be reading this book.
- **Listen.** Sometimes the person with the food and weight concern just needs someone to listen to how they feel. Work at creating opportunities for your loved one to talk about feelings and be willing to listen without judgment to their fears, dreams, and frustrations.
- **Connect.** Try to connect with your loved one as a whole person. See them as someone who has thoughts, feelings, opinions, and experiences beside their eating issues.
- **Take an active role in treatment.** Some research shows that in 90 percent of the cases where the family was involved in treatment, the individual with the eating disorder fully recovered. Eating disorders affect the entire family. When asked, participate in therapy. When

asked to respect your loved one's confidentiality, do so. Remember you did not cause the eating problem. However, your participation and courage to work on you can be part of the solution.

- **Get support for yourself.** Recovery is a long-term process. Most people with food and weight concerns are in treatment for a year or more. During that time, you need to find safe places to get support, to vent your frustrations at the your loved one's problem with food, and to be able to share with others the victories along the road to recovery.
- **Stay hopeful.** Be supportive of your loved one's recovery efforts. Have hope. Recovery is possible.

Eating Disorders Treatment and Referral Centers.

National Organizations

AED Academy for Eating Disorders
6728 Old McLean Village Dr., McLean, VA 22101
(703) 556-9222
www.aedweb.org

ANAD National Association of Anorexia Nervosa and Associated Disorders
P.O. Box 7, Highland Park, IL 60035
(847) 831-3438
www.ANAD.org

Council on Size & Weight Discrimination, Inc.
P.O. Box 305, Mount Marion, NY 12456
(845) 679-1209
www.cswd.org

Harvard Eating Disorders Center
c/o Massachusetts General Hospital WACC-725
15 Parkman Street, Boston, MA 02114
(617) 236-7766
www.hedc.org

IAEDP International Association of Eating Disorders Professionals
P.O. Box 1259, Pelein, IL 61555-1295
(800) 800-8126
www.iaedp.com

MEDA *Massachusetts Eating Disorders Association, Inc.*
92 Pearl Street, Newton, MA 02158
(617) 558-1881
www.medainc.org

National Eating Disorders Association
603 Stewart Street, Suite 803, Seattle, WA 98101
(206) 382-3587 Helpline: 1-800-931-2237
www.nationaleatingdisorders.org

NEDSP *The National Eating Disorders Screening Program*
One Washington Street, Suite 304, Wellesley Hills, MA 02481
(781) 239-0071
www.mentalhealthscreening.org

The Something Fishy Website on Eating Disorders
www.something-fishy.org

Hospitals and Treatment Centers

Children's Hospital Boston
300 Longwood Avenue
Boston, MA 02115
(617) 355-6000

Hampstead Hospital
218 East Road
Hampstead, NH 03841
1-800-600-5311
www.hampsteadhospital.com

Laurel Hill Inn
P.O. Box 368
Medford, MA 02155
(781) 396-1116
www.laurelhillinn.com

Monte Nido
27162 Sea Vista Drive
Malibu, CA 90265
(310) 457-9958
www.montenido.com

Renfrew Center
Centers in Philadelphia, New York, Florida,
New Jesery and Southern Connecticut
1-800-RENFREW
www.renfrewcenter.com

Remuda Ranch
One East Apache Street
Wickenburg, AZ 85390
1-800-445-1900
www.remudaranch.com

The Institute for Living
200 Retreat Avenue
Hartford, CT 06106
1-800-673-2411
www.insituteofliving.com

Waltham Hospital
Hope Street
Waltham, MA 02154
(781) 647-6700

Eating Disorders Resource Catalogues

Brunner-Routledge Books
29 West 35th Street
New York, NY 10001
1-800-634-7064
www.brunner-routledge.com

Gurze Books
P.O. Box 2238
Carlsbad, CA 92018
1-800-756-7533
www.bulimia.com